MW00812521

Enjoy the book... cover to cover !

— Matt Clark

_____

Record Store Day '12

April 21, 2012

#194/250

PUT THE NEEDLE ON THE RECORD

Matthew Chojnacki

FOREWORD BY
Jake Shears *of Scissor Sisters*

AFTERWORD BY
Nick Rhodes *of Duran Duran*

THE
1980s
at **45**
revolutions
PER MINUTE

Other Schiffer Books on Related Subjects:
Rock Posters of Jim Phillips, 978-0-7643-2531-0, $29.95
Great Rock & Roll Street Art, 978-0-7643-2099-8, $29.95

Designed by Justin Watkinson
Cover design by Brian Andrew Jasinski
Type set in Impact/Helvetica Neue LT Pro

ISBN: 978-0-7643-3831-1
Printed in China

Schiffer Books are available at special discounts for bulk purchases for sales promotions or premiums. Special editions, including personalized covers, corporate imprints, and excerpts can be created in large quantities for special needs. For more information contact the publisher:

Published by Schiffer Publishing Ltd.
4880 Lower Valley Road
Atglen, PA 19310
Phone: (610) 593-1777; Fax: (610) 593-2002
E-mail: Info@schifferbooks.com

For the largest selection of fine reference books on this and related subjects, please visit our website at www.schifferbooks.com
We are always looking for people to write books on new and related subjects. If you have an idea for a book please contact us at the above address.

This book may be purchased from the publisher.
Include $5.00 for shipping.
Please visit your bookstore first.
You may write for a free catalog.

In Europe, Schiffer books are distributed by
Bushwood Books
6 Marksbury Ave.
Kew Gardens
Surrey TW9 4JF England
Phone: 44 (0) 20 8392 8585; Fax: 44 (0) 20 8392 9876
E-mail: info@bushwoodbooks.co.uk
Website: www.bushwoodbooks.co.uk

4880 Lower Valley Road Atglen, Pennsylvania 19310

This book is dedicated to the **brain**, the athlete, the basket case, the **princess**, and the criminal.

Thanks for introducing me to new wave music, Mr. Hughes.

Contents

Creative mistakes are almost always just as fascinating as our successes. Someone close to me once likened creating an entirely successful album campaign to trying to hold two handfuls of water. I think he was right.

I remember putting together ideas for my band's first album. All I started off with was the sleeve for Steve Miller's *Book of Dreams*, the amulet on the back of Roxy Music's *Avalon*, and the poster art for the '90s bomb *Showgirls*. Working with a very talented artist named Spooky Tim, we conceptualized a cover that was going to be a woman walking into a portal with a teeming city on the other side. It turned out that implementing this fantasia was going to be a lot harder than anticipated.

For the album cover I also thought of the sleeve for Stevie Nicks' *Trouble in Shangri-La*, since it had a similar set up. I really liked the way her dress flowed out behind her, like a nude-colored bouquet. I found out very quickly that sometimes when you show someone an image for inspiration, they take it as meaning that you want it duplicated. I'll never forget the phone call saying: "You're going to be SO happy with the photos we did of the model from behind. We had Stevie Nicks' dress replicated EXACTLY. You're going to love it!" I

felt defeated. Sure enough, if you hold up the two sleeves side by side, you'll see that the two women are wearing the same dress.

Call me an old lady, but computers have really peed all over music artwork. In the last fifteen years or so, programs like Photoshop have homogenized images, giving us freedom, yet imposing more restraint. The primary battle over our first album cover was to make it look less like it had been made by a computer. Though it is a great sleeve, we didn't entirely succeed.

I'll also never forget looking at the artwork for our first major label single, "Laura." While I loved the image, I couldn't get over the fact that the woman and goat man on the sleeve looked like CGI mannequins. I was mildly horrified at their stiff pose and overly smooth skin.

However, when I look back on what I thought were the faults of all these sleeves, I now realize that it is the imperfections that make them special.

Admittedly, I may not exactly be the perfect person to be talking about twelve-inch art, since by the time I reached early adolescence, records were well on their way out, and compromised plastic cassettes had weaseled their way into my grimy

little hands. However, I do have very distinct memories of sleeves that piqued the interest of my developing little six-year-old brain. One was the twelve-inch sleeve of "Relax" by Frankie Goes to Hollywood. My oldest sister had the vinyl, and I'll never forget connecting that steely fetishistic art with the dangerous-sounding single that I kept hearing on the radio in the back of my mom's car. I remember soon thereafter that the backlash had started, and I saw my sister wandering the house in a white t-shirt with large black and white type that said "UP YOURS FRANKIE," proving that the tides of pop are always turning.

And it seems like they keep turning faster and faster, the latest example being with the iPad on which I am typing this foreword. In one swift move, I believe that suddenly Apple has revived sleeve art. Now when I play LCD Soundsystem's *This Is Happening*, for instance, the black-and-white cover pops up in all of its fuzzy glory. What only yesterday had turned into a thumbnail has now become a third larger than the size of a CD. We always seem to be mourning the loss of the past, but somehow, I feel that what we thought was going to end up missing forever is going to return with a vengeance.

But what makes truly great music art? Maybe there's no secret, but we know it's good when we see it. I made a choice recently with artwork that had a fascinating reaction. For the sleeve of Scissor Sisters' album *Night Work*, we decided to license a Robert Mapplethorpe photograph of a ballet dancer's ass in tights, each cheek being gripped urgently by a pair of hands. The moment I saw it, I knew it had to be the album cover. I also knew that we could follow it with other Mapplethorpe photos for the single sleeves.

As it went to press, I received a phone call from one of the Universal CEOs about the decision to use the image. He told me that by using it, it was going to be one of the worst mistakes I'd ever made in my career. He said that it would alienate people and turn the Average Joe off to the record.

I told him the truly great story of Patti Smith turning in her own Mapplethorpe photograph for the sleeve of *Horses*. Clive Davis, the head of Artista, threw a fit, saying that no woman should appear on an album cover dressed in men's clothes, with undone hair, no make-up, and a moustache. Smith did not relent, thank God, and now Horses is one of the best sleeves of all time. The CEO laughed and told me never to compare him with Clive Davis again. I laughed back and told him to quit acting like him, then.

Sometimes, having success feels like nothing other than having a string of failures peppered every once in a while with good news. Time will tell whether or not *Night Work*'s sales live up to the standards of the record label. But if choosing that photograph sends the record into commercial flop-dom, it'll still be one of the best mistakes I've ever made.

It must be that some of the artists in this book have had similar experiences, and feel as passionate about their sleeves as I am with mine. As you flip through these pages, I hope you can revel in all the possibilities that music artwork has had and will continue to have, for as long as we're listening.

Jake Shears
AUGUST 2010

Introduction

It was the '80s, and this is our story. Punks. Metalheads. New Wavers. Hip-Hoppers. Mall Chicks. Preps. Stoners. Different clothing, slang, and lifestyles with one common bond: a turntable and a stack of vinyl.

Music defined the decade. "Video Killed the Radio Star" ushered in MTV, "Don't You (Forget about Me)" ruled *The Breakfast Club*, and "I Still Haven't Found What I'm Looking For" became the anthem for a generation. However, it wasn't just about the music, it was also about the art of the music. What we saw was nearly as important as what we listened to, and decades later the images of the '80s continue to dominate our culture.

Record sleeves and music videos inspired new and dramatic looks for our self-expressive Me Generation. New Wave artists Annie Lennox and Gary Numan shunned gender stereotypes for androgyny, while Mötley Crüe and Poison turned fashion into hyperbole with body-conscious Lycra, extreme makeup, and outlandish hairdos. On the other end of the spectrum, machismo and street culture ruled as Run-D.M.C. and Sugarhill Gang introduced thick gold chains, Fedora hats, and black sweat suits in what would become the enduring hip-hop lifestyle. Music, lyrics, and fashion, together, expressed who we were or who we wanted to be.

Artists and management quickly observed the societal impact of this imagery and began recognizing the importance and influence of packaging and design when marketing music. From then on, the slipcover of every new recording received almost as much attention as the record it wrapped. Singles were the most common purchase at the time, showcasing seven and twelve-inch artwork that rivaled LPs. Traditional headshots of artists (or in most cases, plain white 45 sleeves) were replaced with unique photographs and graphic design that expressed both the style of the artist and the trends of an era. The music and art worlds collided like never before, with the likes of Madonna, Grace Jones, and Debbie Harry befriending breakout designers and photographers such as Keith Haring, Jean-Michel Basquiat, and Herb Ritts.

However, while an album's artwork lived on, enduring several decades of reformatting (on cassette, CD, and now digitally), the life span of an '80s single was brief. Depending on its success on the charts, each single (and its artwork) vanished from store shelves within a few weeks or months of its release.

The music from these singles lived on, and now, with this book, I'm happy to say that their artwork will as well. I hope the extraordinary cover designs, long-forgotten images, and never-before-heard stories from these defining artists will trigger new memories that last as long as the songs that inspired them.

Drop that needle,
Matthew Chojnacki

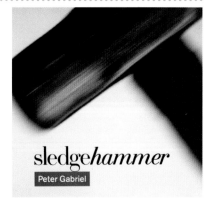

Put the Needle on the Record features more than 250 vinyl single covers, selected from a review of more than 10,000 (including international variations). Artwork is paired based on theme and design, and is from seven-inch vinyl sleeves unless otherwise noted.

A key for each single's caption is on the following page.

Row 1: R.E.M. "Stand" vs. R.E.M. "Get Up"

Row 2: Diana Ross "Swept Away" vs. Shannon "Do You Wanna Get Away"

Row 3: Peter Gabriel "Big Time" vs. Peter Gabriel "Sledgehammer"

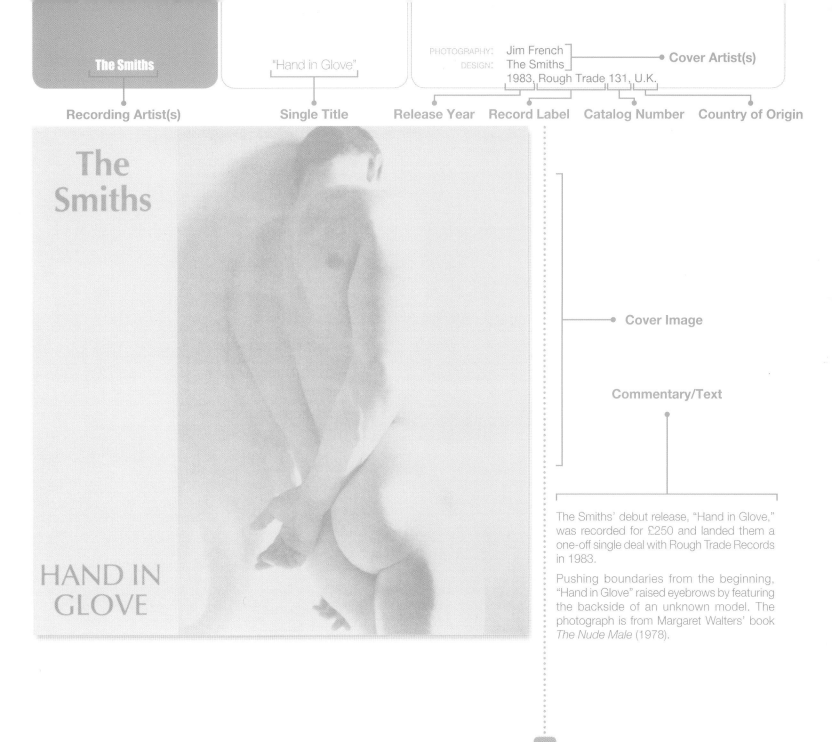

The Smiths

"Hand in Glove"

PHOTOGRAPHY: Jim French
DESIGN: The Smiths
1983, Rough Trade 131, U.K.

Cover Artist(s)

Recording Artist(s) **Single Title** **Release Year** **Record Label** **Catalog Number** **Country of Origin**

The Smiths

HAND IN GLOVE

Cover Image

Commentary/Text

The Smiths' debut release, "Hand in Glove," was recorded for £250 and landed them a one-off single deal with Rough Trade Records in 1983.

Pushing boundaries from the beginning, "Hand in Glove" raised eyebrows by featuring the backside of an unknown model. The photograph is from Margaret Walters' book *The Nude Male* (1978).

Cyndi Lauper's sleeve for "What's Going On," originally by Marvin Gaye, was inspired by artist Man Ray's photograph *Larmes* (*Tears*).

It takes on a new meaning when viewed next to the strikingly similar close-up for "It's Over Now" by Luther Vandross, who passed away in 2005.

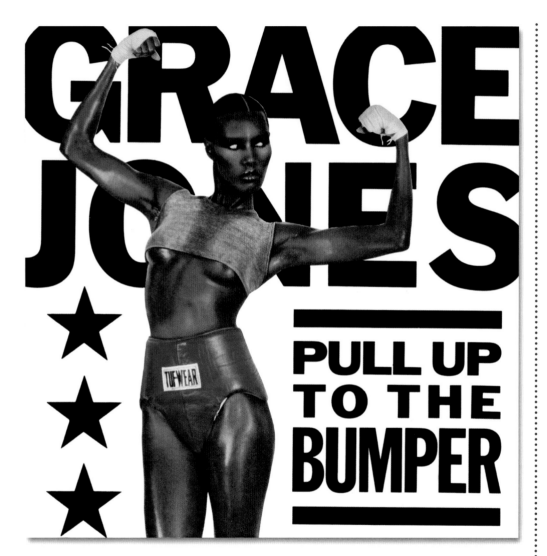

Grace Jones developed cult icon status by challenging racial and sexual stereotypes with her aggressively flamboyant persona. "Pull Up to the Bumper" and ABC's sleeve for "Poison Arrow" reflected the increasingly independent, strong portrayal of women in '80s music.

ABC frontman Martin Fry: "With 'Poison Arrow' we wanted the sleeve to reflect what was inside. The song was all about heartache and defiance and the battle of the sexes. Post punk was dead. We were brand new. Anti rock and roll. We wanted to be shiny and high gloss and glam. Smart and stupid at the same time. Gered Mankowitz was the photographer. He shot it like a classic Powell and Pressburger movie. High saturation, vivid hard colours. The beautiful woman is clearly in the driving seat. She's an assassin. Love is the weapon. The lettering aspires to ad agency branding. ABC as pure product."

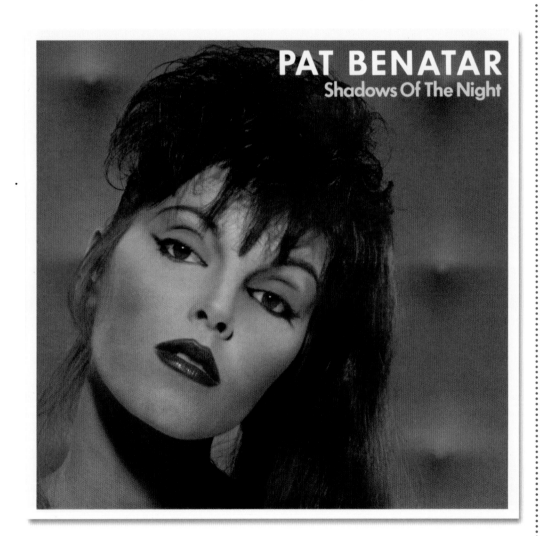

The new wave movement of the late '70s and early '80s generated an androgynous, detached look. Extreme makeup and hair (including the classic asymmetrical cut) were club going essentials.

Rock vocalist Pat Benatar ("Love Is a Battlefield," "We Belong") and electronic music pioneer Gary Numan ("Cars," "I Die: You Die") were early adopters of this new visual wave.

Gary Numan on his striking "Berserker" artwork: "Years before the 'Berserker' cover I saw an article that looked at body painting. They had a series of pictures that featured women painted in various ways and photographed against a suitable background. One was a woman painted like a big cat lying in a tree. Another, the one that helped me with 'Berserker,' was a woman painted as marble, lying on a marble wall. Body painting took me along that particular thought process and eventually to the idea for the white face, blue hair, and the whole 'Berserker' image."

| Def Leppard | "Hysteria" (+ six singles) | DESIGN: Andie Airfix @ Satori
1987–1989, Mercury 870004 (etc.), U.S. / U.K. |

An impressive seven hit singles were released from Def Leppard's *Hysteria*. Each of the single sleeves comprised a portion of the album's cover art. The two final puzzle pieces were sold in a limited edition U.K. box set for "Love Bites."

Hysteria designer Andie Airfix: "Those were the days when record companies stretched the limits of seven- and twelve-inch single formats. Since Mercury Records had confidence in the success of so many singles from the album, they immediately agreed to the puzzle concept."

The pieces: "Hysteria" (row one, center), "Love Bites" (row one, right), "Armageddon It" (row two, left), "Animal" (row two, center), "Women" (row two, right), "Pour Some Sugar on Me" (row three, center), and "Rocket" (row three, right).

Airfix vividly remembers the band's reaction to her artwork, "the band saw my preparatory sketch and absolutely loved it. They wanted to retain a powerful image in line with hard rock, but also to modernize it and avoid the clichés. The head was intended to express dark fears associated with the psychotic state of hysteria. The computer background was one of the first computer-generated graphics. Believe it or not, the image was a black-and-white drawing, fed into a computer, colored very primitively, and then output as an 8 x 10 transparency—essentially a screen shot (hence the screen texture)."

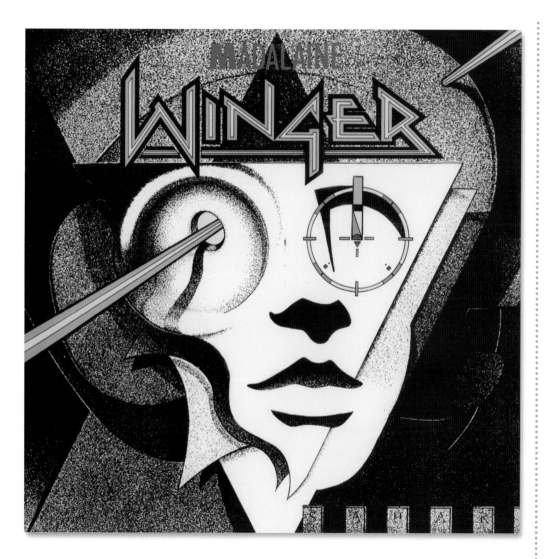

Airfix's design seemingly inspired other artists to create similar pieces, including Winger's "Madalaine."

| The B-52's | "Private Idaho" | PHOTOGRAPHY: Lynn Goldsmith
DESIGN: Robert Waldrop
1980, Warner 49537, U.S. |

Known nearly as well for their audacious fashion sense as for their music, The B-52's and The Romantics shared an interest in retro duds and gravity-defying coifs.

The B-52's name was derived from the beehive hairstyle that resembled the nose of a B-52 bomber (as worn by Kate Pierson and Cindy Wilson), while The Romantics' tag referenced the day that they formed, Valentine's Day 1977.

Fred Schneider on The B-52's visual style: "I hung out with Keith, Ricky, and other friends. We would go to a thrift store called The Potter's House and buy any clothes that struck our fancy, usually shirts from the '50s and '60s (25 cents), and pants (75 cents) that fit…somewhat. Socks were a nickel. We would also buy wild outfits for our gal pals and later bought things for Kate and Cindy when we started to hang with them. When I first met Cindy (at a Halloween party), I wore a seersucker suit, penciled in a mustache, and had a broken cigarette hanging out of my mouth. I went as a hangover. I later had this look for the stage until David Byrne co-opted it, along with a lot of other ideas, for his *Stop Making Sense* movie. To this day we are credited with creating thrift store chic (chic, huh?)

| The Power Station | "Communication" | DESIGN: Montxo Algora 1985, Capitol 5511, U.S. |

During a temporary hiatus of Duran Duran in 1985, two-fifths of the band (John and Andy Taylor) formed The Power Station with Robert Palmer and former Chic member Tony Thompson. Hits included "Get It On (Bang a Gong)" and "Some Like It Hot."

John Taylor on The Power Station's sleeve artwork: "I had seen a piece by Montxo Algora in a book called *Little Blue Book* and nicked it for The Power Station album cover. For the 'Communication' single we approached the artist directly and asked him [to design it]."

While John and Andy Taylor resided at The Power Station, Duran Duran's Simon LeBon, Nick Rhodes, and Roger Taylor formed Arcadia. Following these various side projects, Duran Duran returned for the albums *Notorious* ('86) and *Big Thing* ('88).

By 1988, Duran Duran relied on understated graphic design rather than band photos. John Taylor quips, "We wanted to keep the design work around the *Big Thing* album simple, using primary colours, like Fisher-Price toys and building blocks. How else to represent a title as dumb as that?"

| Kate Bush | "Army Dreamers" | DESIGN: John Carder Bush |
| | | 1980, EMI 5106, U.K. |

Two of music's most distinguished vocalists and lyricists appear here in "autographed" photos.

Designer John Carder Bush (also Kate's brother) on "Army Dreamers": "Have you ever noticed that a lot of the traditional anti-war songs, the ones that have come from soldiers' experience, often have perky little tunes that almost deflect you from the cold reality of the words, and, somehow, this makes their message far more chilling? 'Army Dreamers' is one of those kinds of songs. The cover is an attempt to recreate a '40s soldiers' pin-up girl, an integral part of that dreamy madness that attracts young men to the trappings of war. It's also worth remembering that the wonderful video to the song was hardly seen because it was considered as too violent— such an innocent time!"

Dolly Parton's "I Will Always Love You" was originally released in 1974 and was re-recorded here for *The Best Little Whorehouse in Texas*. Elvis Presley was one of the song's biggest fans, but when he asked Parton to record his own version (and requested half of the publishing rights in return), she judiciously declined the offer. The decision paid off when Whitney Houston's rendering of "I Will Always Love You," from *The Bodyguard* (1992), became the biggest selling female single of all time.

Depeche Mode	"New Life"	PHOTOGRAPHY: Rodney Martin 1981, Mute 014, U.K.

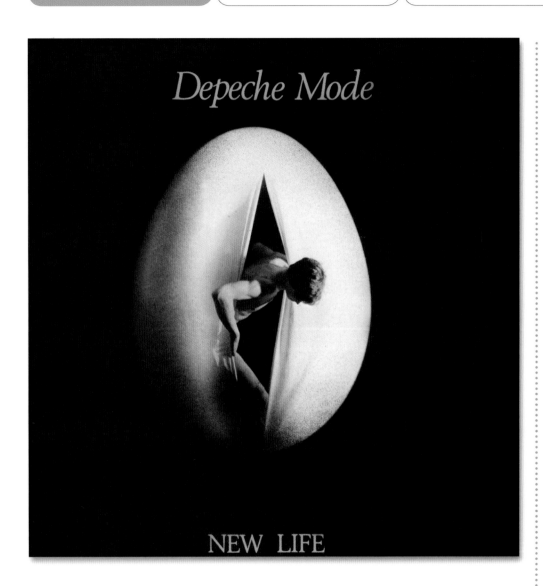

Depeche Mode's "New Life" (featuring a provocative image of an adult birth) and Ultravox's "The Thin Wall" showed the human form "breaking through."

Depeche Mode's initial singles, "New Life," "Just Can't Get Enough," and "Dreaming of Me," reflected the upbeat pop style of then-member Vince Clarke, who penned nearly all of the band's songs. With his departure in 1981 (later forming Erasure with Andy Bell), Depeche Mode moved from their cheery beginnings to a darker, less consumable direction that has since become their trademark.

Ultravox	"The Thin Wall"	PHOTOGRAPHY: Trevor Key DESIGN: Peter Saville 1981, Chrysalis 2540, U.K.

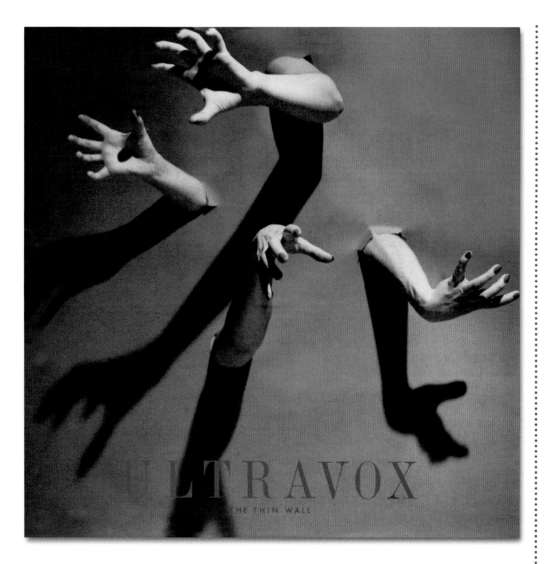

New wavers Ultravox also morphed considerably over time. John Foxx fronted the band in the mid-'70s, followed by Midge Ure, who led the group to over a dozen U.K. Top 40 hits including "Vienna" and "The Thin Wall." Ure later co-wrote "Do They Know It's Christmas?" and hit #1 as a solo artist with "If I Was" (1985).

The Cold War between the Soviet Union and the United States brewed on during the '80s, generating a stream of singles (Men at Work's "It's a Mistake," Sting's "Russians") and feature films (*WarGames*, *Red Dawn*) that addressed the conflict.

| Sigue Sigue Sputnik | "Sex Bomb Boogie" | DESIGN: Sigue Sigue Sputnik / Bill Smith Studio
1986, EMI 201564, Germany |

New wave cyberpunk band Sigue Sigue Sputnik, perhaps best known for "Love Missile F1-11," raised eyebrows in the midst of the Cold War by presenting a disturbing, post-apocalyptic view of society. Gender-bending fetish clothing, towering Mohawks, and extreme makeup accompanied provocative cover artwork.

Sigue Sigue Sputnik was led by bassist Tony James. "I was interested in all forms of graphics, and would tear out strong images that I liked," says James, "everything —books, comics, adverts, to the packaging of Japanese toys. I looked for ideas that strongly branded the concept in the simplest form. Meanwhile, I had seen a picture of a belt with vibrators instead of bullets in a futuristic magazine. EMI generally gave me complete freedom…absolute freedom corrupts?"

Dead or Alive   "I'll Save You All My Kisses"

PHOTOGRAPHY: Paul Cox
DESIGN: Peter Barrett / Andre W. Biscomb
1987, Epic / Burns 3, U.K.

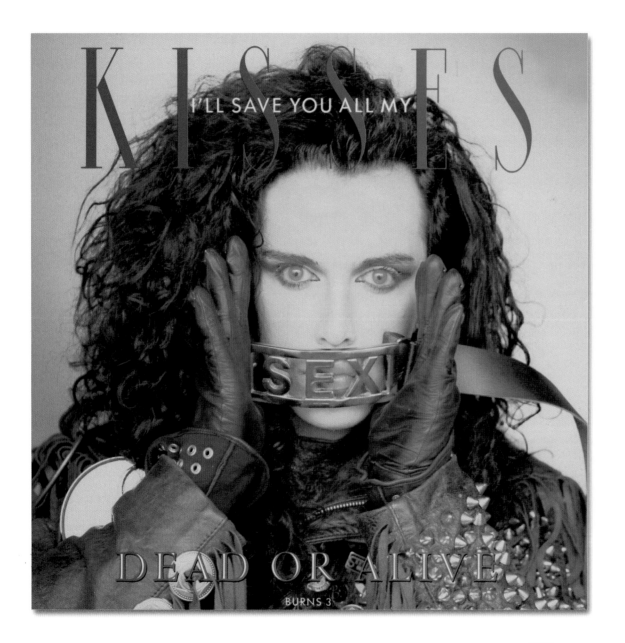

"I'll Save You All My Kisses"

PHOTOGRAPHY: **Paul Cox**
DESIGN: **Peter Barrett / Andre W. Biscomb**
1987, Epic / Burns G3, U.K.

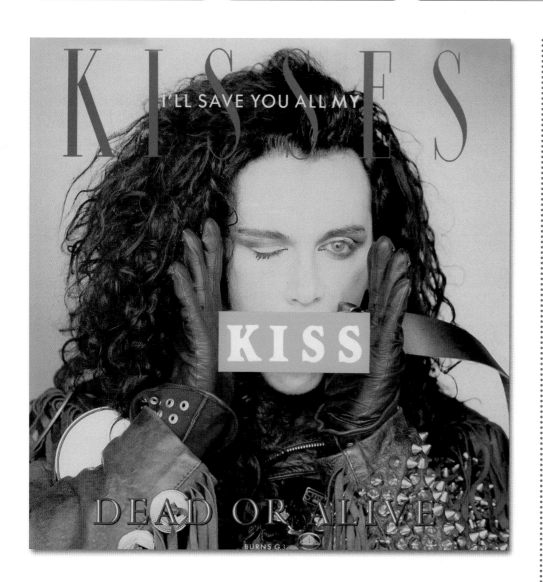

Pete Burns of Dead or Alive blurred sexual boundaries with his larger-than-life, flamboyant personality. Dead or Alive had a series of dance hits including "You Spin Me Round (Like a Record)" and "Brand New Lover."

"I'll Save You All My Kisses" (the fourth single from Dead or Alive's *Mad, Bad, and Dangerous to Know* LP) had several different sleeves, one of which was censored by skittish retailers. The altered single had a "KISS" sticker covering Pete Burns' tongue, which probed through his "SEX" belt buckle in the original photo.

The related video, featuring Burns in black tights, a studded leather jacket, and a metal codpiece, was banned by MTV in several territories due to its sexual overtones.

Sugarhill Gang	"Rapper's Delight"	DESIGN: Unknown
		1979, Sugar Hill 310816 {12"}, France

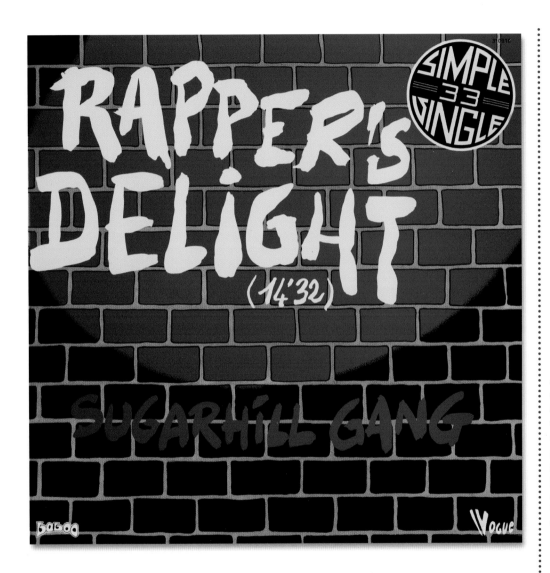

In the early '80s rap was viewed as little more than a fad; singles were produced inexpensively and with little attention to sleeve design.

However, the Sugarhill Gang's "Rapper's Delight" signaled the beginning of the hip-hop era by becoming the first rap single to reach the Top 40 in the U.S. The single, which sampled Chic's "Good Times," was only available as twelve-inch vinyl since it clocked in at a lengthy fourteen minutes, thirty-two seconds.

| Kurtis Blow | "The Breaks" | DESIGN: Unknown
1980, Mercury 4010 {12"}, U.S. |

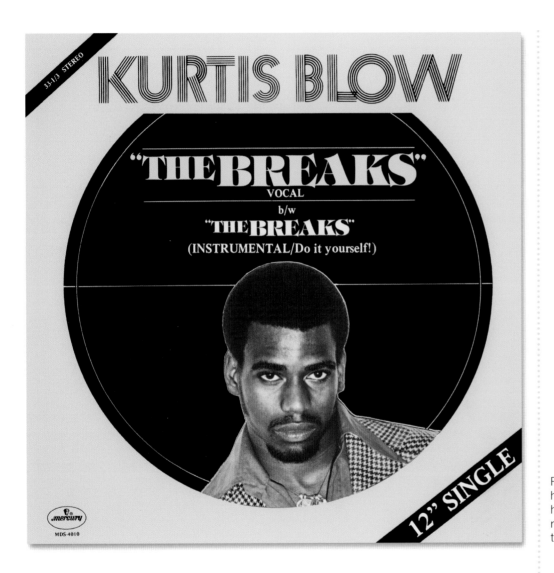

Rap pioneer Kurtis Blow followed, and made hip-hop history by being the first rapper to have a gold single ("The Breaks"), a major-label record deal (Mercury), an international concert tour, and an endorsement deal (Sprite).

Thomas Dolby

"She Blinded Me with Science"

DESIGN: Thomas Dolby / Andrew Douglas
1982, EMI / VIPS 104, U.K.

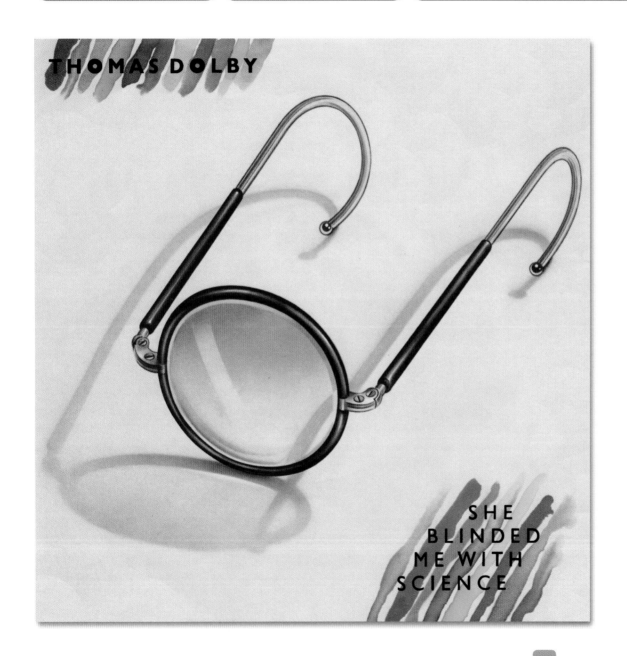

THOMAS DOLBY

SHE
BLINDED
ME WITH
SCIENCE

I →0■ AM →1■ A →1A■ CAMERA
20 44 211
CAR 2075

BUGGLES

Optical illusions were used on Thomas Dolby's "She Blinded Me with Science" and the Buggles' "I Am a Camera." Both synth pop artists led the "geek is chic" movement by bringing science and technology to the forefront in music.

Dolby on his "Science" artwork: "The mono-spectacle idea came from photographer Andrew Douglas (of Douglas Brothers fame), whom I used to brainstorm with on everything visual. He had a great archive of clippings from various eras, and he showed me an early-20th-century Dada object that was a single horn-rimmed spectacle. So we adapted this artwork from a photo of my own specs at that time. I guess what's funny about it is that your imagination creates an image of the strange mutant that must wear such an item. The original is probably in a museum somewhere, alongside that steam iron with the nails in it."

Guns N' Roses	"Paradise City"	ILLUSTRATION: Andy Engell / Bill White, Jr.
		DESIGN: Michael Hodgson
		1989, Geffen 27570, U.S.

Robert Williams' 1978 painting *Appetite for Destruction* (used for the Japan-only *Live* EP [opposite]) served as the original cover art for Guns N' Roses' eponymous groundbreaking album. However, protests from women's groups and Tipper Gore's Parents Music Resource Center (PMRC) pressured Geffen to replace it with an image of a skull-covered cross. The revised cover was also used for the "Paradise City" single, as shown here. Williams explains that he initially urged Axl Rose to choose another one of his pieces, since *Appetite for Destruction* was "a little too radical for the mainstream. But I figured that this was just another punk band that wanted some wild shit."

Williams continues, "So, low and behold, this band just takes off. Just fucking takes off. And that's all I hear about in the news, that they have trouble with the album cover. It was just upsetting everybody." Williams found himself the center of a media circus, defending himself on MTV and in the press. "They came back and wanted another album cover, and I said 'just fucking forget it,'" says Williams. "The public thinks that any time you're connected with a star, you're hot. They paid me almost fucking nothing. But the bad thing is that the painting was never realized for what it was. It was a super cartoon for the underground art galleries. It was breaking away from pop art. I've come up with a magazine called *Juxtapoz* for that kind of art and now it's accepted."

The wildly opposite facial features of Swing Out Sister's Corrine Drewery and The Cure's Robert Smith were emblematic of their respective bands, with Swing Out Sister being the more jovial crew.

Drewery, a former fashion designer, explains that "Breakout's" cover photograph "wasn't originally intended to be a record sleeve at all. It was from a session for [British fashion lifestyle magazine] i-D. i-D covers always feature people with one eye closed to match the i-D logo. If you turn it on its side it is a big grin with the right eye winking. We were thinking of ideas for the 'Breakout' sleeve and this photo seemed to convey the mood of the song perfectly." Drewery continues, "I was in such a sense of panic. The success of this, our second single, would decide whether or not we would go on to sign an album deal, and as usual I had left completion until the night before the deadline. Looking back, I suppose the lyrics were somewhat autobiographical. I had wanted to be a singer since I was three years old, but my dreams were diverted for awhile."

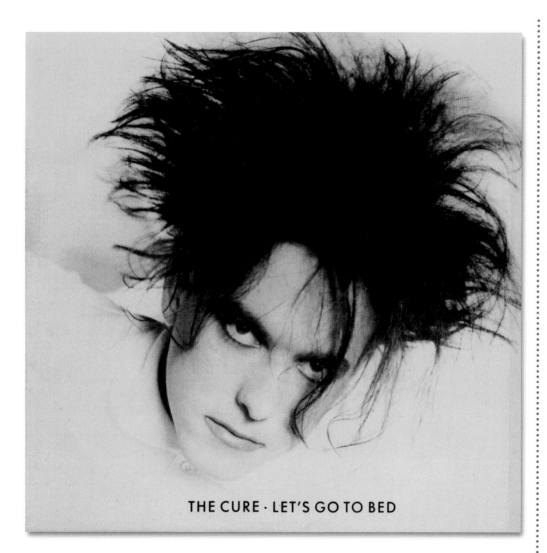

THE CURE · LET'S GO TO BED

Contrasting Swing Out Sister's cheer is Robert Smith, who unofficially led the goth movement with his uninhabited hair and (normally) smudged lipstick. The Cure's roster of gloomy and introspective songs included "Boys Don't Cry" and "Lovesong."

Madonna	"Everybody"	ILLUSTRATION: **Lou Beach**
		DESIGN: **Christine Sauers**
		1982, Sire 29899 {12"}, U.S.

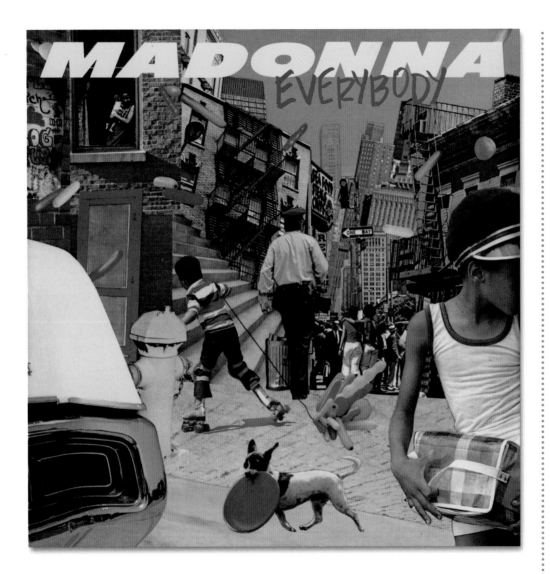

Madonna's "Everybody" depicted New York's Lower East Side/East Village, while "This Is England" portrayed a Brit city landscape.

"Everybody" was Madonna's first commercial single and originally appeared on the four-track demo that landed her at Sire Records. Madonna famously signed her Sire contract at the hospital bedside of label president Seymour Stein, who was impressed by her work ethic and determination.

Without her image on the "Everybody" cover, many disc jockeys assumed, then unknown, Madonna was African-American. It was an instant dance floor smash, the first in an endless series of club anthems for Madonna.

"Who knew?" says "Everybody" cover artist Lou Beach. "I never think about the longevity of a project when I'm working on it. I just wanted to convey a feeling of the streets, teeming with people."

| The Clash | "This is England" | ILLUSTRATION: Eddie King |
| | | 1985, CBS 6122, U.K. |

While Madonna pushed the boundaries of pop music, The Clash established itself as the definitive British punk band, with its fiery stage presence and rebellious, political lyrics. "This is England" was The Clash's first single from their final LP *Cut the Crap*.

Adam and the Ants	"Stand and Deliver"	PHOTOGRAPHY: Allan Ballard
		DESIGN: Jules Balme / Adam Ant
		1981, CBS 1065, U.K.

Initially a punk band, Adam and the Ants reinvented themselves as swashbuckling pirates with a penchant for tribal rhythms. The overhaul was a quick success, and "Stand and Deliver" became their first U.K. #1.

Longtime Adam Ant designer Jules Balme describes first meeting Adam: "Although I'd seen loads of Ants gigs, I didn't meet him until the eve of the single "Kings of the Wild Frontier." It was in the corridors at CBS and I remember saying something like 'I know you do all your sleeves but if you ever need a hand...' He phoned me the next week. He had it all worked out and knew exactly what he wanted, and as a result, was a great client to work for. Given that this was also the era of 'my girlfriend has done a drawing for the sleeve,' Adam's professionalism was a welcome relief."

| Bow Wow Wow | "I Want Candy" | DESIGN: **Unknown**
1982, RCA 238, U.K. |

The Ants subsequently moved to another group that was forming, Bow Wow Wow. After a six-month search for a lead vocalist, Bow Wow Wow discovered 15-year-old Annabella Lwin at a dry cleaner. She stirred controversy by appearing partially nude on some of the band's sleeves, including the early MTV staple "I Want Candy."

Roxette's "Neverending Love" and The Korgis' "Everybody's Got to Learn Sometime" both contained quirky, retro graphics.

"Neverending Love" (Roxette's first single) was deliberately designed to exclude head shots of the famous duo. Per Gessle explains: "The single sleeve (without a Marie/Per picture) was made to confuse everybody about Roxette. Both Marie and I had domestic careers going and we had the homegrown idea that if the track didn't make it, nobody would have noticed that it was us. But, God was good and it was a huge hit in Sweden. Soon afterwards I managed to persuade Marie to record a full album based on a Swedish LP that I was writing at the time. I translated most of the songs into English and off we went."

The Korgis struck a nostalgic vibe with the sleeve for their unconventional hit "Everybody's Got to Learn Sometime."

Vocalist James Warren: "At the time we were signed to a small independent label, Rialto, and the MD [managing director] was very keen to establish a distinctive artwork profile for all the single and album covers. Fortunately his art and design man, George Rowbottom, had a terrific eye for all things quirky and kitsch, and it was he who came across a wonderful collection of obscure 1950s American advertising pictures. These chimed perfectly with the slightly weird retro aesthetic of The Korgis, and George's excellent designs graced all three of the band's album covers and (I think) most of the singles."

| Pet Shop Boys | "Love Comes Quickly" | PHOTOGRAPHY: Eric Watson
DESIGN: Mark Farrow @ Three Associates / Chris Lowe
1986, Parlophone 12R6116 {12"}, U.K. |

Bros	"Too Much"	PHOTOGRAPHY: John Stoddart
		DESIGN: Three Associates
		1989, CBS / ATOM T7 {12"}, U.K.

Homoerotic imagery hit the mainstream with sleeve artwork such as Pet Shop Boys' "Love Comes Quickly" and Bros' "Too Much."

Longtime Pet Shop Boys photographer and video director Eric Watson details his history with the band, as well as the "Love Comes Quickly" imagery: "Neil Tennant and I were friends for a number of years in London. After I finished studying at Hornsey College of Art we collaborated on a book about the band Madness, who had just released a film. This was seen by the staff at *Smash Hits* magazine and we were both invited to work for them." At about the same time Neil met Chris Lowe at a hi-fi shop in Chelsea, London, forming Pet Shop Boys.

For "Love Comes Quickly," Watson says that he "didn't want eyes in the shot. We were all playing a game in which the record company was being given less and less typographical information on the covers. There is beauty in the simply presented. The Japanese do this extraordinarily well and I think this beauty has its roots in humility."

Regarding sleeve cues to Pet Shop Boys' sexuality over the years: "Everything was done in an arch manner, when you know something and you don't really discuss it. You just power ahead and see what you can get away with. Imagine if we'd saved the 'Love Comes Quickly' portrait and put it on the cover of 'Rent' instead. That would have made 'obviously out' seem like an understatement. When I think about it, 'Rent' was 'renty' enough anyways. Two puffs at Kings Cross. Oh dear."

Van Halen	"Jump"

ILLUSTRATION: Margo Zafer Nahas
ART DIRECTION: Pete Angelus / Richard Seireeni / David Jellison
1984, Warner 929384, France

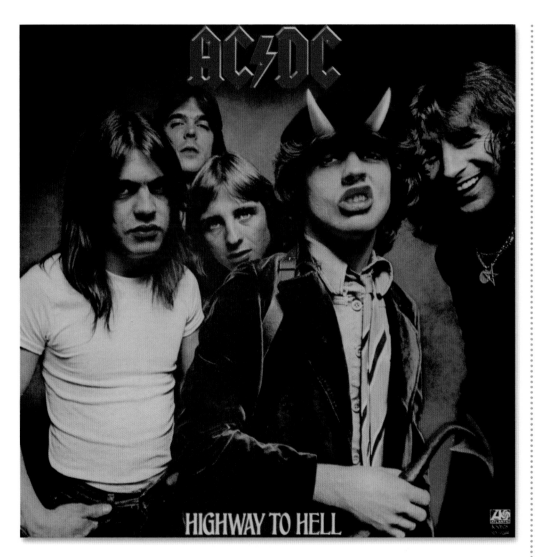

Two of music's most enduring rock bands, Van Halen and AC/DC, had a knack for using head-turning cover artwork.

Artist Margo Nahas painted Van Halen's iconic *1984* LP sleeve (also used for the "Jump" single). "The band had a somewhat nebulous idea having to do with four dancing chrome women," says Nahas. "I was known at the time for my photo-realistic air brush prowess, especially my ability to render shiny metal (a staple in rock cover art). As the group looked over my work, they came across a painting I had done for myself, a baby angel smoking a cigarette. It was kind of love at first sight."

"I asked my friend if I could take some photos of her 2-year-old son," continues Nahas. "I styled his hair, gave him some candy cigarettes, and after a brief tantrum he became the perfect character. The cigarettes were chocolate, wrapped in paper to look like the real thing, and Carter Helm, my little model, ate every one of them."

Nahas was taken back by the widespread exposure of her piece. "I remember at the time being surprised by its popularity. The cover was omnipresent. Everyone was aware of the image whether they were a fan of Van Halen or not," says Nahas. "I never imagined then, when I created the image, that Van Halen would buy the rights for an album cover, or that album art could be iconic, or that there would be books published on record artwork. It's just great."

| Rock Steady Crew | "Uprock" | ILLUSTRATION: Doze Green |
| | | 1984, Charisma / Virgin RSC 2, U.K. |

In the late '70s, break dancing was virtually unknown outside of New York subculture. Rock Steady Crew was instrumental in bringing the dance form to an international stage. The group was featured in the underground hip-hop films of the time, including *Wild Style* and *Style Wars*, as well as in more mainstream fare such as *Flashdance* and *Beat Street*.

Mantronix	"Needle to the Groove"	ILLUSTRATION: **Gemini & Gnome**
		ART DIRECTION: **Studio Zed**
		1985, Sleeping Bag 00015 {12"}, U.S.

Mantronix's "Needle to the Groove" similarly helped to pave the way for hip-hop, inspiring a generation of musicians including Beck; the robotic line "two turntables and a microphone" can be heard on Beck's "Where It's At" single.

"Uprock's" graffiti artwork was designed by one of its original members, Doze Green, while "Needle to the Groove's" cover was created by New York underground graffiti artist legends Gemini & Gnome.

MLVC

LIKE
A
PRAYER

specially priced maxi-single

Christopher Ciccone, artist and graphic designer for Madonna's Blonde Ambition and The Girlie Show tours (and also her brother), painted the twelve-inch artwork for "Like a Prayer."

"The Catholic Church was my first great influence," explains Ciccone. "The piece was specifically created for the single. It was also at a time when my paintings held heavy religious overtones, as did the song. Madonna wanted something that would reflect those things, while being relatively subtle at the same time. It was more than anything a personal note from me to Madonna. I chose to use her initials [MLVC = Madonna Louise Veronica Ciccone] and the unnamed saint to retain my creative needs while making clear that it was her record. The floating 'P' over the body of the saint was my acknowledgement of her relationship to Sean Penn at the time."

Even though the sleeve did not feature Madonna's (marketable) image, Sire didn't hesitate with the artwork. "The record company had no influence," says Ciccone, "Madonna didn't require label approval for her covers, and she has always been smart enough to surround herself with people who could illuminate her significant gifts."

| OMD | "Maid of Orleans" | DESIGN: Peter Saville |
| | | 1981, Dindisc 40, U.K. |

Also theologically based, the stained glass-style of OMD's "Maid of Orleans" referenced Joan of Arc, French heroine and saint of the Roman Catholic Church. The song was from OMD's befittingly titled album *Architecture and Morality*.

| Paul Hardcastle | "19" | PHOTOGRAPHY: John Bryson / Image Bank
DESIGN: John Pasche / Stephen Horse
1985, Chrysalis 2860, U.K. |

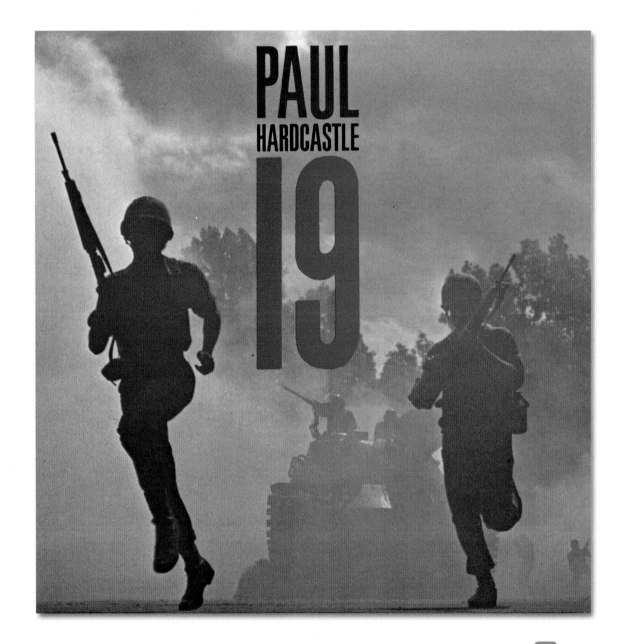

| R.E.M. | "Orange Crush" | PHOTOGRAPHY: **U.S. Navy**
1989, Warner 2960, U.K. |

Vietnam was revisited with Paul Hardcastle's "19" and R.E.M.'s "Orange Crush." Both used actual military photos as covers. "19" spoke about Post-Traumatic Stress Disorder by combining clips of news reports and testimonials over a synth beat, while "Orange Crush" referenced the U.S. military's use of the defoliant Agent Orange.

"I was watching a television documentary, *Vietnam Requiem*, and had taped it on Betamax," explains Hardcastle. "I thought that the subject was interesting for a record, the main idea being that soldiers were just 19. It was either going to be a massive hit or a mega failure, but I'm glad I stuck to my guns. Chrysalis was very nervous."

Following "19's" success, Hardcastle received "hundreds of letter from Vets, who used '19' as their theme whilst marching through Washington."

Hardcastle's manager at the time was Simon Fuller, who later became the acclaimed producer of *American Idol*. Fuller named his production company, 19 Entertainment, after the Hardcastle hit.

| Queen | "Body Language" | DESIGN: Unknown
1982, EMI 5293, U.K. |

QUEEN

BODY LANGUAGE↑⇇

While Queen had little difficulty in Europe with their suggestive "Body Language" sleeve, the U.S. had two altered releases.

The first edition removed the female's posterior, but nevertheless was deemed too provocative for stateside audiences. A subsequent version censored the image completely and had a plain white cover. Since the white sleeve was tremendously less popular, it became one of the rarest and most valuable Queen collectibles.

The accompanying video clip also caused a stir for its sexual and homoerotic overtones, and became one of the first videos banned by MTV. *Body Language* director Mike Hodges: "After the '60s the U.K. was much more liberal than the U.S. (where I assume the decision was made). America was very much in the grip of Puritanism, so, in retrospect, it's not so surprising MTV banned it."

Hodges continues, "I directed *Flash Gordon* in 1979/80 and we had Queen do the music. I spent 21 days—and nights —intermittently with all four of them. Each member composed different themes for different sections of the film. We became friends, I directed the video for the film's title music, and *Body Language* followed directly from that. I also seem to recollect that it [the single cover] was a still from the shoot."

"Freddie was a charmer," says Hodges, "hyperactive and incredibly talented—not just musically but also in the visual arts. Needless to say, he was very involved in the video's concept. I was merely the interpreter."

Hodges called it quits as a video director after the controversy. "I enjoyed making *Body Language* simply because of Freddie and Queen. But I really didn't fancy making other music videos—not that I was asked to. Besides, once he clip was banned it was, of course, never seen!"

| Freddie Mercury | "I Was Born to Love You" | DESIGN: **Unknown** |
| | | 1985, CBS 43604, Brazil |

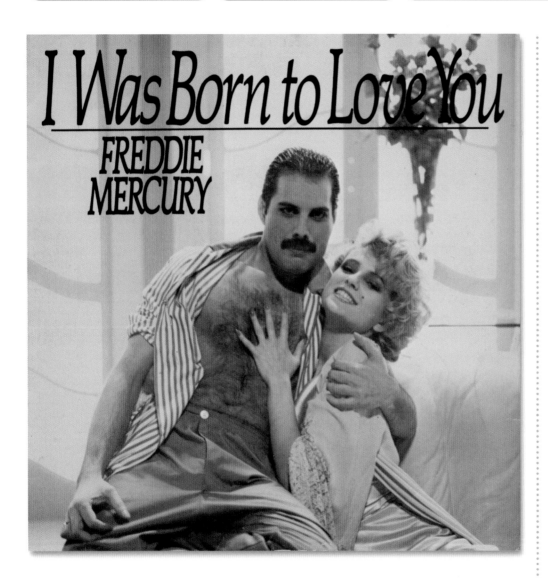

This rarely seen sleeve for Freddie Mercury's "I Was Born to Love You" showcased Mercury's sense of humor, with Mercury and Debbie Ash posed in a theatrical, Rhett Butler meets Scarlett O'Hara black-and-white shot. The Brazil-only cover has become one of the most sought-after collectibles among Queen fans.

"I Was Born to Love You" was originally released for Mercury's first solo LP (1985's *Mr. Bad Guy*). Queen re-recorded it a decade later for their *Made in Heaven* album following Mercury's untimely passing in November 1991.

Also posed in a nostalgic black-and-white shot is Missing Persons' Dale Bozzio. "Give's" dramatic cover was lensed by fashion photographer Helmut Newton (*Playboy, Vogue*). His erotic, detached style was the perfect marriage with new wave music.

Missing Persons' other hits included "Words, Destination Unknown" and "Walking In L.A."...all in regular rotation during MTV's early days.

| Talking Heads | "And She Was" | PAINTING: Rev. Howard Finster
DESIGN: M & Co.
1985, Sire 28917, U.S. |

| Tom Tom Club | "Genius of Love" | ILLUSTRATION: James Rizzi |
| | | 1981, Island / WIP 6735, U.K. |

Renowned folk artist Rev. Howard Finster painted the cover for Talking Heads' "And She Was." His artistic style was similar to the intricate, urban creations of former New York cabby James Rizzi, who drew Tom Tom Club's "Genius Of Love" sleeve.

Tom Tom Club was a side project for Talking Heads' Tina Weymouth and Chris Frantz, and Rizzi was a friend of the couple's.

"Chris and Tina had taken me to the Bahamas for the recording of the single," says Rizzi. "So, the cover art, which was not based on an existing piece, was very much influenced by their music and the beautiful setting of the Bahamas."

The music video for "Genius of Love" brought Rizzi's drawings to life. "If I remember correctly, this was the first fully animated music video ever, and we were under a tight schedule. We only had thirty days to finish it, and worked day and night. This was in the days before computer animation, so everything had to be hand-drawn, twenty-four images per second of the clip's duration." That's three minutes and twenty seconds, or approximately 4,800 sketches!

Elton John's last single of the '80s, "Healing Hands," was a tribute to '60s soul music, while Eurythmics' "Thorn in My Side" was written as an icy cast-off to a former lover. Both contained hand-guarded head shots.

No stranger to pushing boundaries with their music and video clips, Eurythmics generated double-takes with their cover artwork as well.

Annie Lennox discusses the importance of sleeve imagery: "The intimate association between sound and vision can create a powerful and profound potentiality. Images inform and assist in guiding you to whatever message is contained within the music. We exist in a universe of information which is constantly being processed and deciphered by our senses and intellect. As an artist, I've always relished the opportunity to explore ideas and prod the boundaries. Having freedom to express oneself via the broad arena of 'pop culture,' incorporating the photographic image, symbol and metaphor, word, melody, rhythm, movement, texture, composition, social commentary, style, sex, drama, angst, ecstasy...in fact...the total range of human emotion and experience can be encountered in the process."

Frankie Goes to Hollywood	"Relax"	ILLUSTRATION: Yvonne Gilbert
		DESIGN: XLZTT
		1983, ZTT / ZTAS 1, U.K.

"relax don't do it
when you want to
suck it to it
relax don't do it
when you want
to come!"

RELAX
FRANKIE GOES
TO HOLLYWOOD

Frankie Goes to Hollywood

"Relax"

ILLUSTRATION: Yvonne Gilbert
DESIGN: XLZTT
1983, ZTT / 12 ZTAS 1 {12"}, U.K.

"relax don't do it
when you want to
go to it
relax don't do it
when you want
to come!"

BBC disc jockey Mike Read famously broke a copy of Frankie Goes to Hollywood's "Relax" on the air, branding it "disgusting" after seeing the single cover (which originally included the incorrect lyric "suck it to it"—see the seven-inch sleeve opposite). The BBC later banned the record. The initial "Relax" video was also refused and required two re-shoots due to homoerotic imagery.

"Relax" subsequently flew off of store shelves, becoming the second best-selling '80s single in the U.K., bested only by "Do They Know It's Christmas?"

"I think the uproar was cleverly managed," says cover artist Yvonne Gilbert, "but when punk and bondage fashions had already taken to the streets it's a little disingenuous to be shocked by a video. I am dead against any form of censorship (barring children and animals), and it amazes me what people profess to be shocked by."

Gilbert explains how the cover art came together: "I knew Holly [Johnson] and Paul [Rutherford] from our Liverpool days. So Holly knew my work. Although as an illustrator I mostly earn my living from drawing princesses and dragons, I love to work on erotic images and have spent some time working for *Playboy* and *Men Only*, and at the same time was working on fetish illustrations. I like to draw both men and women but am careful never to make women the victims of the piece. In fact, it is usually the other way around!"

"I was glad the image was such a success but it was somewhat galling to see it reproduced all over the place, in every country, and get nothing from it," says Gilbert. "I sold the rights for a nominal fee, and that was it. I remember a lot of dreadful rip-offs, too, which tickled me. However, there is some comfort in the fact that it is still recognized."

| Madness | "Our House" | PAINTING: **Karen Allen**
 1982, Stiff / Buy 163, U.K. |

Peter Max? Andy Warhol?

No…Karen Allen, age six.

When Madness sought the ideal image for their "Our House" single, they rang up a local primary school asking for student artwork. Little Karen Allen's piece was deemed the perfect fit for the now-classic single.

| Michelle Shocked | "When I Grow Up" | ILLUSTRATION: **Lindsay Namm**
DESIGN: **Sheryl Lutz-Brown / Helen Namm**
1988, Mercury 872590, U.S. |

Michelle Shocked similarly nabbed a kid Picasso for her "When I Grow Up" single.

Designer Helen Namm explains, "At the time my daughter Lindsay was about six years old and was always bringing drawings home from school. One day she came home with a portrait that she said was of me. I loved it and brought it to work [at Polygram] to hang on my wall. When it came time to create the sleeve for the single, it just made sense to use her drawing. The art sold for $200 and it was immortalized!"

Lindsay retired as an in-demand artist on top of her game. "She graduated college and went on to work in the business world" instead of continuing with art, says Namm.

Dark yet witty, genuine yet complex—Fad Gadget (a.k.a. Frank Tovey) was the avant-garde first signing of Mute Records, later home to a host of popular electronic acts including Yazoo, Depeche Mode, and Erasure. While never landing on the charts like his contemporaries, Fad Gadget was an underground sensation, a notable pioneer in the early days of industrial and electronic music.

Fad Gadget's cover artwork reflected Tovey's often confrontational personality. This was particularly apparent live, where Tovey would often injure himself from his intense performances.

| Tin Machine | "Under the God" | DESIGN: Unknown
1989, EMI 2237, Australia |

tin machine

under the god

David Bowie began on a similarly rebellious path beginning in the '70s. However, by the late '80s Bowie had adapted a mainstream sound and image, causing him to fall out of favor with many fans and critics.

Tin Machine was Bowie's attempt to take a step back into his darker fare. The band had a hard, metallic sound, and Bowie returned to his roots by playing small clubs and venues. "Under the God" was a decent-sized hit, and the band's first LP received generally positive reviews. However, by 1993 Bowie downsized to a solo artist once again for his *Black Tie, White Noise* LP.

Duran Duran	"Rio"	ILLUSTRATION: **Patrick Nagel**
		DESIGN: **Malcolm Garrett**
		1983, Capitol 5215, U.S.

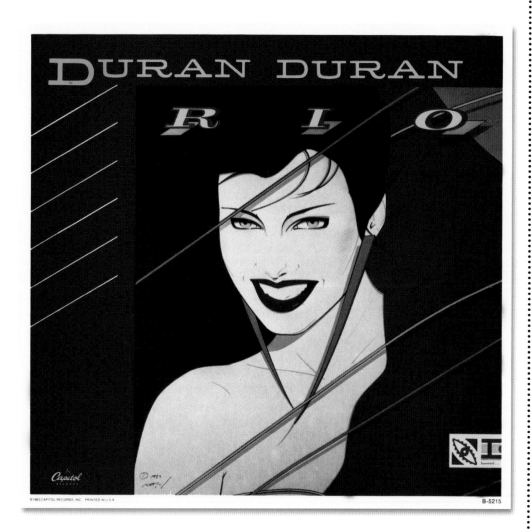

Art deco sleeves such as "Rio" and "Drive" were commonplace not only as vinyl covers, but also as framed artwork in the '80s.

Artist Patrick Nagel ("Rio") was internationally recognized for his elegant and stylish focus on the female form. He would typically begin with a photograph and remove the intricate elements until a flat image remained.

Duran Duran's John Taylor: "We had seen Nagel's illustrations in *Playboy* magazine, and approached him off the back of that. He did two designs for us and we chose the one (on the 'Rio' cover). Then the other one appeared out of the blue on the Japanese single release of 'My Own Way.' No one had told the Japanese label that we had not actually bought that one."

Simon LeBon: "'Rio' was always special to me. I do recall that I mostly spent the next two years, after the record was released, trying to locate and procure a girlfriend who looked like the one in Nagel's picture on the cover."

| The Cars | "Drive" | PAINTING: Peter Phillips
1984, Elektra 69706, France |

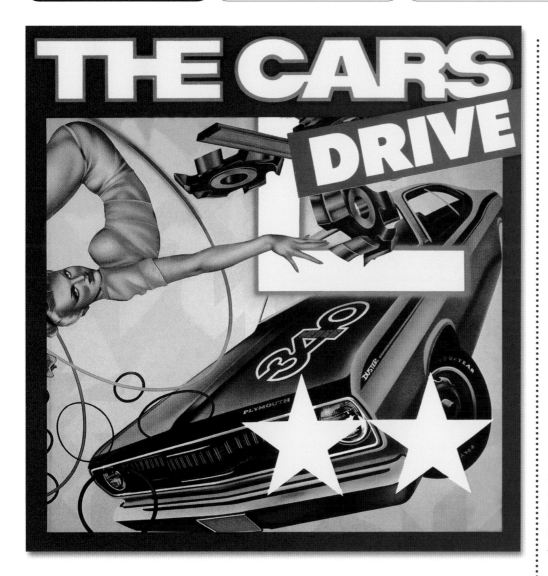

Pop artist Peter Phillips ("Drive"), sometimes referred to as the British counterpart to America's Andy Warhol, juxtaposed familiar societal images into his collages and paintings. The "Drive" cover (featuring a '71 Plymouth Duster 340) was from Phillips' 1972 piece *Art-O-Matic Loop di Loop*.

Platinum Blonde	"Somebody, Somewhere"	PHOTOGRAPHY: Dimo Safari
		DESIGN: Hugh Syme
		1985, Columbia C4-7127, Canada

Australia's INXS and Canada's Platinum Blonde designed sleeves that saluted the mail art movement of the '50s to '90s, which used the postal service as a medium. Both "I Send a Message" (an early INXS hit) and "Somebody, Somewhere" were fully functional envelopes that contained vinyl 45s.

Platinum Blonde's Mark Holmes: "The sleeve was an attempt to send a letter to the fans… with some goodies inside. It soon turned into a nice work of art. I've always loved creative album graphics and feel very lucky to have one of our own for the ages. Hugh [Syme, design] and Dimo [Safari, photography] were so creative and cared very much about the band."

Holmes reflects back on the decade: "The '80s were a time of great parody and ridicule about the hair and clothing choices, but we were lucky enough to be in a decade when these things were happening for the first time. Much like the '50s, '60s, and '70s, the '80s relied on the present rather than just making music and fashion that reflected on another time period. The '90s to now have been about a little bit of everything from those decades. Who would have known at the time that the '80s was the last original progression?"

While "It's Raining Men" winked at gay life in the '80s, Josie Cotton took a more direct approach with "Johnny Are You Queer?"

"I paid dearly for that song," explains Cotton. "[Queer] was a taboo word that people weren't used to hearing in a public forum. Girls falling for beautiful gay boys was a real cultural phenomenon. The time was right and the world was ready…well, at least we thought it was! I had no idea that the religious right would take up a crusade against me, or that I would be banned in Amsterdam, or that certain factions of the gay community would go after me relentlessly as they did."

Cotton initially wanted to push the cover artwork a bit further. "Bomp Records' original artwork was a bit more provocative, to say the least. They had Johnny coming out of a gay bathhouse. Johnny had a rainbow of colored bandanas in the back pocket of his short shorts. In the '80s each colored bandana was Morse code for your sexual preferences. I thought it was genius but my producers were aghast upon seeing it for the first time. I will never forget the looks on their faces. It was priceless!"

In retrospect, Cotton is pleased with "Johnny." "It was featured on the compilation *A Date with John Waters* (a record of disturbing love songs for the ages), so I feel completely vindicated at this point. The great thing is that the gay community now owns the word [queer] and I'm very proud to have been a small part of making that happen."

The Clash

"Rock the Casbah"

PHOTOGRAPHY: Peter Ashworth
DESIGN: Jules Balme
1982, CBS 2479, U.K.

English rockers The Clash and The Kinks had unlikely pop hits with "Rock the Casbah" and the nostalgic "Come Dancing."

Clash designer Jules Balme: "I'd known Kosmo Vinyl (Clash PA, PR, and A&R man) since I was at college. We had developed a great working relationship since he involved me with The Clash, just after *London Calling*. The creation of this single was a case of 'Jules, get your paint brush out again.' It took me about an hour to paint [the 'Rock the Casbah' sleeve] and an hour for Peter to shoot."

"['Rock the Casbah'] was unusual in that the band were less and less involved with the packaging by then," explains Balme. "The concept came from Bernie [Rhodes, Clash manager]."

The sleeve also set the tone for the accompanying low budget, controversial video clip, which featured a sheikh and a rabbi dancing together while The Clash performed in front of an oil well.

The Knack	"My Sharona"	DESIGN: Doug Fieger 1979, Capitol 4731, U.S.

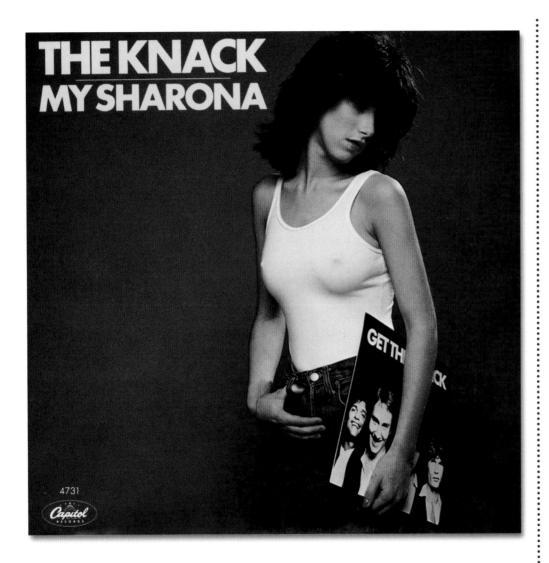

When The Knack's lead singer/guitarist Doug Fieger met Sharona Alperin, she inspired an extended period of songwriting for Fieger, including the band's debut single, "My Sharona." "That was the real Sharona [on the cover]," stated Fieger.

The iconic single has been covered numerous times, including takes by Nirvana and Veruca Salt. However, "'Weird Al' Yankovic's parody ['My Bologna'] is probably my fave," said Fieger, who also thought that the song's use in *Reality Bites* was "fun and well done."

PHOTOGRAPHY: B. Leloup
DESIGN: Claude Caudron
1985, Record Shack / SOHO 34, U.K.

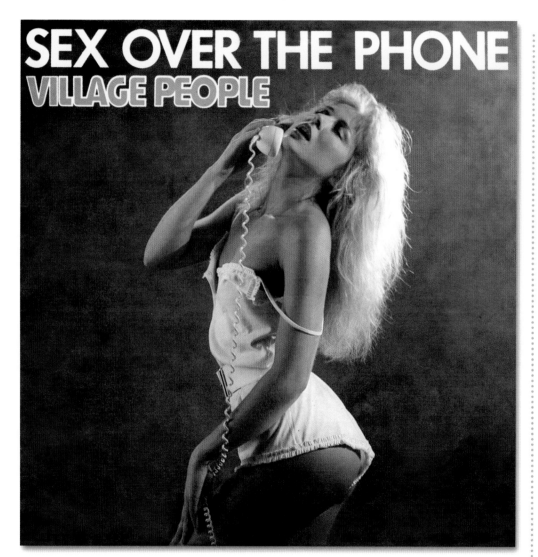

SEX OVER THE PHONE
VILLAGE PEOPLE

Perhaps taking a cue from Fieger's cover design was Village People's "Sex over the Phone." The song was co-written by comedic scribe Bruce Vilanch in response to the rampant phone sex trends at the time.

"I got friendly with [producer] Jacques Morali," says Vilanch. "We had written a song for Eartha Kitt, 'Where Is My Man?,' which was a big disco hit. Jacques called me—over the phone!—and suggested the title for a new song for the Village People and I ran with it."

Vilanch continues: "For Jacques, the joke was that he was writing about all-American things as the Army, the Navy, and the YMCA. He also felt the decline of the Village People began when he mistakenly wrote and produced a song called 'sleazy' and premiered it on *20/20*. He says the bottom began falling out about then. Of course, disco was also ending, and the movie [*Can't Stop the Music*], which I am proud to announce I wrote the first draft of (I quit before there was a second), was a turd. The only place it was a success was Australia, where disco was peaking, for reasons no one but Priscilla Queen of the Desert could ever explain."

| Emanon | "The Baby Beat Box" | ILLUSTRATION: **Keith Haring**
1986, Pow Wow 7403 {12"}, U.S. |

Artist and social activist Keith Haring emerged in the early '80s inspired by New York City life alongside friends and artists such as Jean-Michel Basquiat, Grace Jones, and Madonna.

Haring's instantly recognizable bold lines and active figures covered the gamut—birth and death, love and sex, peace and war. Haring initially found a presence in NYC subways (his "laboratory" for experimentation), creating as many as forty large, chalk drawings a day for millions of commuters to view.

By the mid-'80s Haring was an international sensation, appearing in numerous group and solo exhibitions, creating designs for companies such as Swatch and Absolut vodka, and lending imagery to charitable campaigns (e.g., *A Very Special Christmas*).

On rare occasion, Haring designed cover artwork for musicians that he admired, including disco icon Sylvester (of "You Make Me Feel [Mighty Real]" fame) and Emanon, Doug E. Fresh's beat-boxing protégé.

Haring passed away in 1990, but his imagery and activism lives on.

Longtime friend Madonna paid extensive homage to Haring's work during her 2008–2009 Sticky & Sweet tour (notably during "Into the Groove"). Madonna spokesperson, Liz Rosenberg: "It certainly goes without saying that Madonna's feelings about Keith, as well as his art work, are heartfelt and passionate. Her homage to him, and the early '80s when they spent time together, was so apparent in the show [Sticky & Sweet]."

Ratt	"Ratt"	PHOTOGRAPHY: Neil Zlozower
		LEGS: Tawny Kitaen
		1983, Time Coast 2203 {12"}, U.S.

Prior to releasing their breakthrough LP, *Out of the Cellar*, glam metal band Ratt emerged with a self-titled, independently released EP.

The sleeve featured the rodent-covered legs of rock model Tawny Kitaen. At the time she was dating high school sweetheart (and Ratt guitarist) Robbin Crosby.

| Michael Jackson | "Dirty Diana" | PHOTOGRAPHY: Sam Emerson
ART DIRECTION: Tony Lane / Nancy Donald
1988, Epic 07739, U.S. |

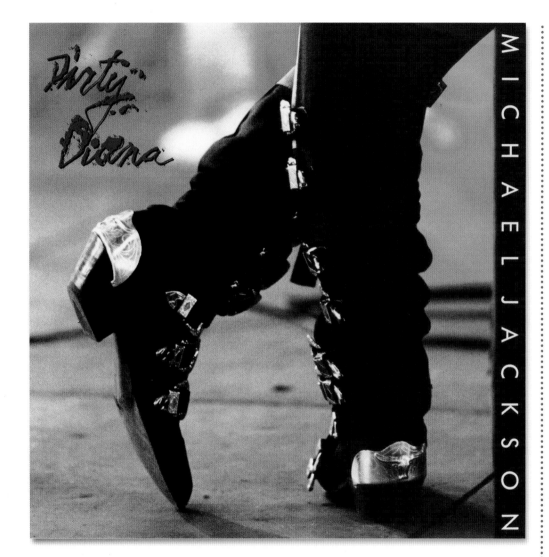

MICHAEL JACKSON

Opposite are the instantly recognizable, trademark boots of pop icon Michael Jackson. "Dirty Diana" was the fifth and final U.S. #1 from the *Bad* LP, following "I Just Can't Stop Loving You," "Bad," "The Way You Make Me Feel," and "Man in the Mirror."

Contrary to urban legend, the song was not about Diana Ross or Princess Diana, but was rather about an obsessed groupie. However, when Jackson played Wembley in 1988, with Princess Diana in attendance, he cut the track from the concert, thinking that she might be insulted.

It was instead one of Princess Diana's favorite tracks.

| **New Order** | "Blue Monday" | DESIGN: Peter Saville |
| | | 1983, Factory / FAC 73 {12"}, U.K. |

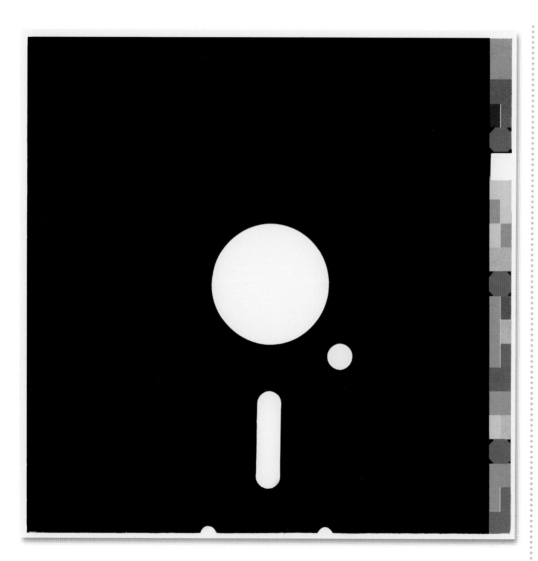

Electronic music pioneers Kraftwerk foresaw the '80s home computer revolution with "Computer Love." They were one of the first acts to use purely synthetic, electronic sounds in their recordings, from diverse sources as a Texas Instruments Speak & Spell to a Mattel Bee Gees Rhythm Machine.

While "Computer Love" recalled the look of an early-'80s PC (including the monochromatic screen—think Apple IIe), "Blue Monday," by influential dance group New Order, was die-cut to look like a floppy disk.

New Order sleeve designer Peter Saville was so minimal in his approach that he typically did not even include New Order's name or their song titles in his designs. His intention was to suggest a sense of secrecy about the recordings, yet be instantly recognizable to fans "in the know."

| Donnie Iris | "Do You Compute?" | DESIGN: Unknown
1983, MCA 52230, U.S. |

Jerry Buckner and Gary Garcia delighted millions of quarter-popping arcade fans worldwide with "Pac-Man Fever." The jingle-writing duo thought to record the song after becoming Pac-Man junkies themselves.

"All major labels passed on the song, so we released the single independently," says Buckner. "The radio requests were tremendous, with some stations even playing it twice an hour. CBS then sent an executive to meet us. He didn't quite understanding the hype, but when his kid flipped out over the song, they knew they had something."

"The song was a global bestseller," explains Garcia, "we even recorded a Japanese version called 'Puck-Man Fever.'" Decades later the arcade anthem lives on. "We were featured in the *New York Times*' crossword puzzle, on Jeopardy as an audio daily-double, and were mentioned by Homer on *The Simpsons*. Not bad for a couple of yokels from Akron, Ohio," chuckles Garcia.

The sound effects used on "Pac-Man Fever" were recorded directly off of a Pac-Man arcade game, as was the image for the cover.

Opposite is Donnie Iris' "Do You Compute?," which featured Atari 2600-style graphics.

| Simply Red | "Money's Too Tight (to Mention)" | DESIGN: Dennis Morris
1985, Elektra / EKR 9, U.K. |

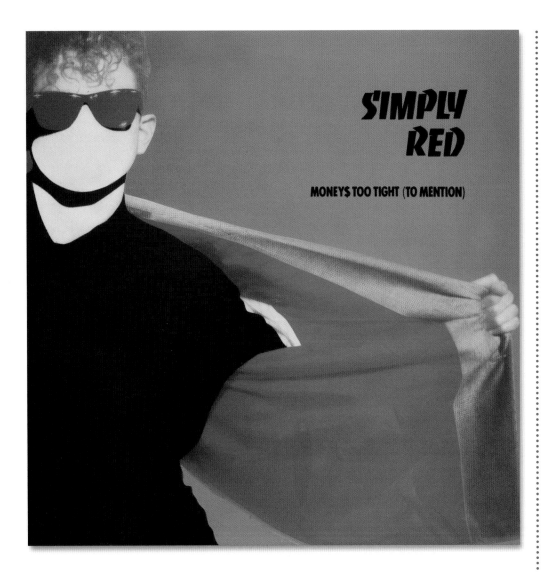

Simply Red and The Human League (pre-"Don't You Want Me" fame) both had "exposed" graphic art for their "Money's Too Tight (to Mention)" and "Empire State Human" sleeves.

Simply Red photographer/designer, Dennis Morris: "Purely by chance, I met [lead singer] Mick Hucknall at the legendary Hacienda club in Manchester. I was hanging out with my friend, the late genius Martin Hannett [Joy Division/New Order producer]. Mick approached me, saying he was a fan of my photography and my band Basement 5. He had just signed a deal with WEA and was hoping to work with me. We spent the rest of the evening together discussing music. Back in London, WEA contacted me, and we had a meeting to discuss budget and ideas...[one] problem being that Mick was not photogenic. So, I decided to make use of his impressive red hair, and bought a red suit to create a striking visual image."

Similarly faceless is "Empire State Human." Human League founding member Martyn Ware explains that the group "regarded the visual representation of the band as highly as the music. When we signed our deal we insisted to have control over both the record and the visuals. The songs were all intended to paint pictures in the mind, and we were all fans of surrealism—Dalí, Magritte, etc. For 'Empire State Human's' sleeve, we decided on a photo session with [Human League musician] Ian Marsh's dad, since he was a builder."

Ware continues, "The lyrics were mostly by Philip [Oakey]. I remember him coming into the studio and mentioning that if someone were to arrive from space the only thing that they would see would be the Great Wall of China. From that description came Phillip's lyrics. Our goal was to make it timeless and not nail it to the current moment, so that it would work in twenty years time. Early Human League was just plain martian, I think. It still sounds pretty unusual."

Journey	"Who's Crying Now"	ILLUSTRATION: Stanley Mouse
		DESIGN: Jim Welch
		1981, Columbia 02241, U.S.

| Asia | "Heat of the Moment" | ILLUSTRATION: Roger Dean |
| | | 1982, Geffen 50040, U.S. |

Heat Of The Moment

The cover artwork for bands such as Journey (here with their scarab beetle mascot) and Asia was often more recognizable than photos of the actual band members. Poster-sized versions of these and other covers were a bedroom wall essential in the '80s.

Asia's John Wetton: "Roger [Dean, illustrator] is an amazing artist, and paints from knowledge of his subject from the inside out. For instance, if he is painting a creature (like the dragon from Asia) he will research the nearest living equivalent, so that he knows the bone/muscle structure, etc., and his research into the history/mythology is equally thorough."

Wetton continues, "[in 'Heat of the Moment'] there are some references to the ethos of the band, 'you catch the pearl and ride the dragon's wings' was written as Roger was preparing the final painting. 'The pearl' is the Pearl of Wisdom, which the dragon is attempting to ensnare.'"

"Heat of the Moment" has certainly lived on since '82, popping up in several videos games, television shows (e.g., *South Park*), and on the big screen. "I think it was particularly great to see it being used in *The 40-Year-Old Virgin* (2005)," says Asia's Geoff Downes. "Apart from *Heat* being used in the prime slot in the film, there were a number of tongue-in-cheek references to Asia throughout the movie. It no doubt helped to raise a new awareness for the band."

Journey has also lived on strong. Rock anthems including "Don't Stop Believin'," "Any Way You Want It," and "Faithfully" still thrive internationally on the radio.

| Stevie Nicks | "Rooms on Fire" | **PHOTOGRAPHY:** H.W. Worthington III |
| | | 1989, Atlantic 99216, U.S. |

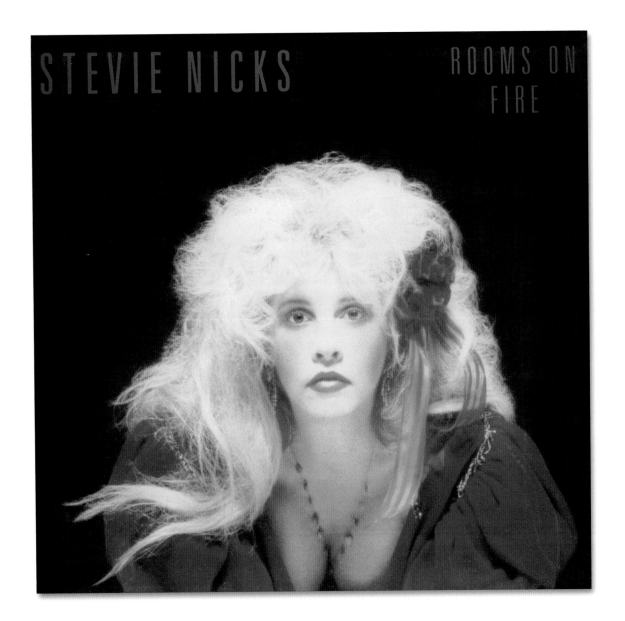

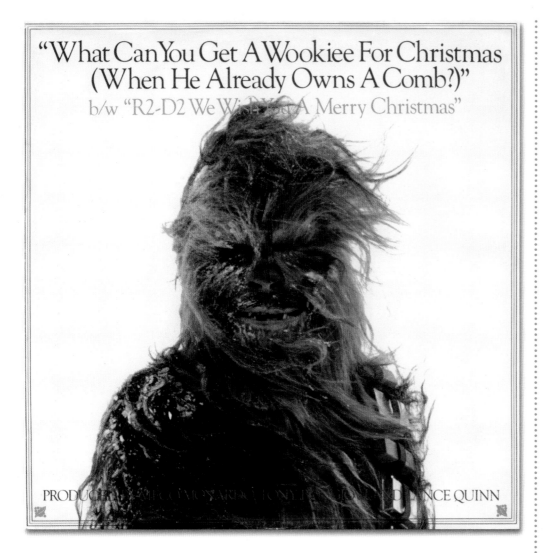

"What Can You Get A Wookiee For Christmas (When He Already Owns A Comb?)" b/w "R2-D2 We Wish You A Merry Christmas"

PRODUCED BY MECO MONARDO AND TONY BONGIOVI AND LANCE QUINN

Stevie Nicks and Chewbacca defined '80s "big hair" with their sleeves for "Rooms on Fire" and "What Can You Get a Wookiee for Christmas (When He Already Owns a Comb?)."

The Chewbacca single was one of several instrumentals composed by Meco, who scored a #1 hit three years prior with a disco version of the *Star Wars* theme.

"In the summer of '80 I had the idea for a *Star Wars* children's Christmas record [including the 'Chewbacca' single] and wrote a long letter to George Lucas," says Meco. "Much to my great surprise, he called me and we spoke for over an hour. RSO Records quickly agreed to the deal and I gathered my team for the LP *Christmas in the Stars*."

Meco tapped a future '80s favorite as a studio singer for the project. "I was unhappy with the singers who attempted 'R2D2 We Wish You a Merry Christmas.' Then my co-producer, Tony Bongiovi, suggested we try his young cousin, Jon. And the rest, as they say, is history, as his rendering of that song became Jon Bongiovi's first recording. From that inauspicious start, and with a slight name change, he went on to tremendous success with Bon Jovi."

Bon Jovi

"You Give Love a Bad Name"

PHOTOGRAPHY: Mark Weiss
1986, Mercury / PRO 434-1 {12"}, U.S.

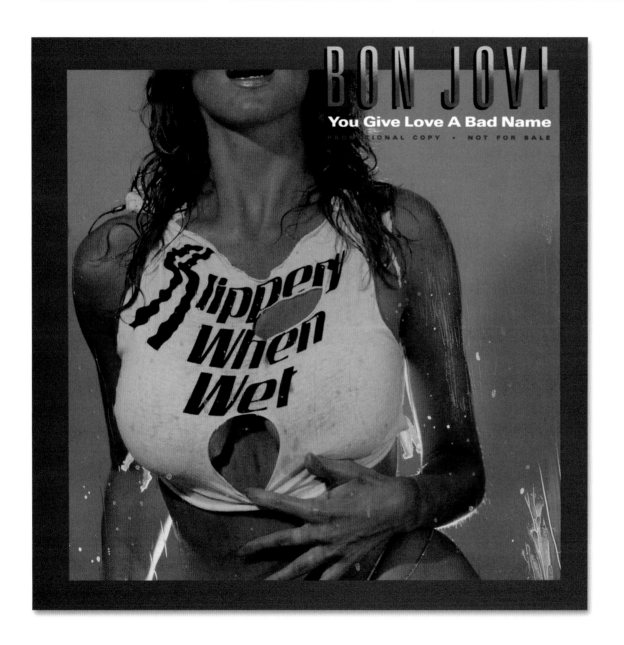

Bon Jovi	"You Give Love a Bad Name"	PHOTOGRAPHY:	Mark Weiss
		ART DIRECTION:	Pete Angelus / Richard Seireeni / David Jellison
			1986, Mercury 884953, U.S.

Originally slated to be the album cover for *Slippery When Wet*, the busty wet t-shirt close-up shown here was rejected as being too racy for retailers. This original sleeve (and the final *Slippery* LP artwork) were both also used to promote the "You Give Love a Bad Name" single.

Photographer Mark Weiss: "We did the shoot for the original back cover (of girls washing cars) in Belmont, New Jersey. We then decided to use one of the girls for the cover—a sexy shot—Jon's idea. Everything was great, everyone loved it, and the label printed the sleeves. That was at about the time that the PMRC was coming down on everybody, and we had to come up with something new over fears that some retailers would not carry the album. The original sleeves, stocked in a warehouse, were all destroyed. One of the new ideas was a girl with a bar of soap labeled 'slippery when wet,' but it didn't work."

"So, Jon called me about a month later. He said, 'We have to come up with something now. I'm on my way.' He drove up to my studio in New York and it was raining out. Jon just said, 'have a Hefty Bag?' I found one, propped it up, but still didn't know what Jon was doing. 'You got a spray bottle, Mark?' Jon sprayed the bag and wrote 'slippery when wet' with his hands, and left. I just took a few shots. I said 'that's it?' 'Yep, see you later man.'"

"When I first met Jon around *7800° Fahrenheit*, Jon said 'I can't believe that I'm shooting with fucking Mark Weiss. You shot everybody.' I said 'one day, you'll be big and fucking not return my calls.'"

Jon still picks up the phone.

"Stereotype"

Harry Truman Doris Day Einstein South Pacific Joe DiMaggio Red China Johnny Joe McArthy Richard Nixon Television North Korea South Korea Marilyn Monroe H. Bomb Rosenberg The King & I Sugar Ray Billy Joel Catcher In the Rye Eisenhower Liberace We Didn't Start The Fire Vaccine Joseph Stalin Allan Carr N.A.S.A. Rockefeller Prokofiev Rock Around The Clock James Dean Davy Crockett Peter Pan Billy Joel Elvis Presley Disneyland Bardot Budapest Alabama Krushchev Princess Grace Trouble in the Suez We Didn't Start The Fire Kerouac Sputnik Bridge on the River Kwai Lebanon Charles de Gaulle Baseball Buddy Holly Ben Hur Space Monkey Mafia Hula Hoops Castro Billy Joel Homeless Vets Tuscany We Didn't Start the Fire Rock 'n' Roll and Cola Wars U2 Kennedy Chubby Checker Psycho Hemmingway Eichman Stranger in a Strange Land Berlin Dylan Lawrence of Arabia British Beatlemania John Glenn Malcolm X JFK Birth Control Billy Joel Ho Chi Min Woodstock We Didn't Start The Fire Watergate Punk Rock Ronald Reagan Palestine Heavy Metal Suicide Wheel of Fortune Foreign Debts Communist Block Billy Joel Rock Around the Clock Prokofiev Rockefeller N.A.S.A. Joseph Stalin Allan Carr Vaccine Liberace Eisenhower Sugar Ray We Didn't Start The Fire Catcher in the Rye The King & I Rosenberg H. Bomb Marilyn Monroe South Korea North Korea Television Richard Nixon Billy Joel Joe McArthy Johnny Ray Red China Joe DiMaggio South Pacific We Didn't Start The Fire Doris Day Harry Truman Rock 'n' Roll and Cola Wars Tuscany Homeless Vets Castro Hula Hoops Mafia Billy Joel Space Monkey Ben Hur Buddy Holly Baseball California Charles de Gaulle Prokofiev Rockefeller N.A.S.A. Joseph Stalin Allan Carr Vaccine Liberace Eisenhower Sugar Ray We Didn't Start The Fire Catcher in the Rye The King & I Rosenberg H. Bomb Marilyn Monroe South Korea North Korea Television Richard Nixon Billy Joel Joe McArthy Johnny Ray Red China Joe DiMaggio South Pacific We Didn't Start The Fire Doris Day Harry Truman Rock 'n' Roll and Cola Wars Tuscany Homeless Vets Castro Hula Hoops Mafia Billy Joel Space Monkey Ben Hur Buddy Holly Baseball California Charles de Gaulle Lebanon Bridge on the River Kwai Sputnik We Didn't Start The Fire Kerouac Trouble in the Suez Princess Grace Krushchev Alabama Budapest Bardot Disneyland Elvis Presley Peter Pan Billy Joel Davy Crockett James Dean Einstein We Didn't Start The Fire Communist Block Foreign Debts Wheel of Fortune Palestine Heavy Metal Suicide Ronald Reagan Punk Rock Watergate Woodstock Ho Chi Min Birth Control JFK Malcolm X John Glenn British Beatlemania Billy Joel Lawrence of Arabia Dylan Berlin Stranger in a Strange Land We Didn't Start The Fire Kerouac Sputnik Bridge on the River Kwai Lebanon Charles de Gaulle Baseball Buddy Holly Ben Hur Space Monkey Mafia Hula Hoops Castro Billy Joel Homeless Vets Tuscany We Didn't Start the Fire Rock 'n' Roll and Cola Wars U2 Kennedy Chubby Checker Psycho Hemmingway Eichman Stranger in a Strange Land Dylan Lawrence of Arabia British Beatlemania John Glenn Malcolm X JFK Birth Control Billy Joel

Ska revival band The Specials and singer-songwriter Billy Joel grabbed attention with a very simple sleeve concept —nothing but type.

While The Specials' sleeve was blanketed with the band's name, Billy Joel's jacket for "We Didn't Start the Fire" contained the single's (lengthy) lyrics.

Joel, a history buff, linked over 120 historical events that took place in his life with the "We didn't start the fire" refrain, rebutting criticism that the Baby Boomer generation was responsible for much of the world's woes. Its style was similar to the stream of consciousness writing of Bob Dylan's "Subterranean Homesick Blues" and R.E.M.'s "It's the End of the World as We Know It (and I Feel Fine)."

Depeche Mode

"Get the Balance Right!"

DESIGN: Martyn Atkins / David Jones
1983, Mute / 7BONG 2, U.K.

"Get the Balance Right" was Depeche Mode's seventh single. Its sleek graphic design stood out in an era of busy and excessive record imagery.

Designer Martyn Atkins: "I used to run sleeve ideas by Dave [Gahan] in those days. DM didn't have a manager so each of the guys had an area of the band's affairs to deal with. It was great. No bullshit third parties to deal with."

"The colours for the sleeve came from my favourite chocolate bar at the time, the 'Milky Bar.' Graphically I was trying to make the cover very mechanical and European in a Kraftwerk kind of way. The little men on the sleeve were doctored from a letraset catalogue, with the hammers giving a nod to the *Construction Time Again* LP cover that we had designed."

"I remember going to show the band the finished artwork for the cover at a film studio in Chiswick, I think, while they were shooting the video for the song. In between takes we consumed large amounts of beer and the cover was approved!"

The Atlantics

"Lonelyhearts"

PHOTOGRAPHY: **Stu Chernoff**
DESIGN: **M & Co.**
1980, Alltime Records, U.S.

Perhaps the perfect companion piece to "Get the Balance Right" was "Lonelyhearts" by Boston faves The Atlantics. The incredibly intricate sleeve featured miniature photographs of the band.

Guitarist Fred Pineau: "Every pose was different. We spent many hours in a New York City photographer's studio while he shot a seemingly endless series of positions from each one of us. You tend to become very creative after you run out of your stock poses, which took place about ten minutes into the process. We were down by the United Nations building and finally got out around 3:00 AM, right when the bars were closing. People were all over the streets, and it was like falling down the rabbit hole in *Alice in Wonderland*. There was a mix of disco divas, punks, dweebs, and people from a gay biker bar called the Headhunter—the sign was painted in bones over the club and there were maybe fifty or so huge Harleys lined up at the curb. There is only one New York."

GRACE JONES: *My Jamaican Guy / J. A. Guys (Dub)*

Eurythmics	"Revival"	PHOTOGRAPHY: Jean-Baptiste Mondino
		DESIGN: Laurence Stevens
		1989, RCA 9904017 {12"}, Brazil

Both Grace Jones and Annie Lennox continuously broke the visual mold for women in the '80s, commanding attention with their rotating guises.

Originally dubbed "the white Grace Jones" by journalists, Annie Lennox went from androgyny in *Sweet Dreams*, to full male drag in the *Who's that Girl?* video, to being a scantily-clad trollop with *I Need a Man*.

However, perhaps nobody changed her appearance as much as Grace Jones herself. Wendy & Lisa (of Prince And The Revolution fame) worked with Jones on her '08 *Hurricane* album and discusses one such transition.

Lisa Coleman: "Grace is one of a kind. One of our favorite stories is a simple one. Once we were all working at the house in our comfy musicians-at-home-in-the-studio clothes. Then Grace got a call reminding her that she had to be at a dinner party. She asked us to drive her there. She had no makeup on and was wearing an odd combination of stretchy clothes and scarves. In the car on the way to the restaurant, Grace transformed herself into a striking art piece icon with just one black eye pencil. She shaded her eyes and used black kohl on her lips. She tied the scarves up and around, this way and that way...and rose from the car a ROCK STAR! We were slack jawed, reeling at the sight of the one and only Miss Grace Jones running from our pumpkin chariot into the glamorous Hollywood night."

"Incidentally, the song to come out of that recording session was 'Williams' Blood,'" says Coleman.

| Dire Straits | "Money for Nothing" | PHOTOGRAPHY: | Brian Aris |
| | | | 1985, Vertigo / DSTR 10, U.K. |

Despite the well-known "I want my MTV" slogan in Dire Straits' "Money for Nothing," Dire Straits lead Mark Knopfler did not support music videos at the time of the single's release. Knopfler thought that videos might have a negative effect on the music industry, and instead wanted to focus on performing.

With a bit of convincing, Knopfler hesitantly agreed to a computer-animated clip for "Money for Nothing." The video ironically earned Dire Straits an MTV Video of the Year Award, besting a-ha's *Take on Me*, among others.

On the opposite end of the spectrum, Sigue Sigue Sputnik frontman Tony James fully embraced the notion that visuals were taking over the industry. "My quote at the time was 'the sound of television is the Jimi Hendrix of the '80s,'" says James. The group's single, "21st Century Boy," had television sets arranged in the form of a cross. "I looked at television as the new religion. The cover was a natural progression. I met Bono years later, who told me that U2 had been very influenced by the Sputnik's vision."

The band further pushed boundaries by having paid advertising interludes in their music, unheard of at a time when music and advertising rarely intersected.

Thompson Twins

"Doctor! Doctor!"

PHOTOGRAPHY: Peter Ashworth
ART DIRECTION: Alannah Currie
DESIGN: Andie Airfix @ Satori
1984, Arista 9209, U.S.

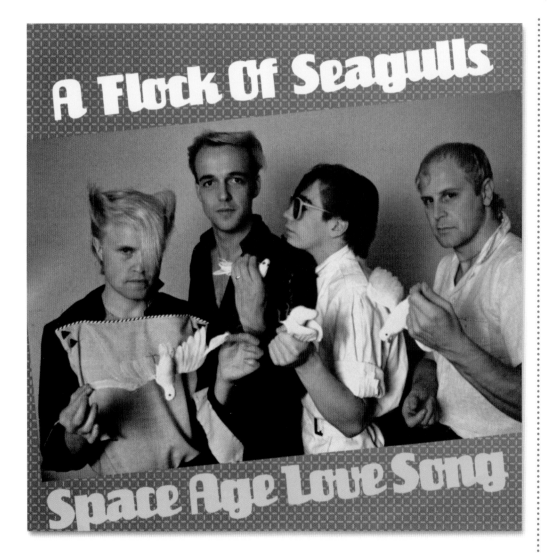

A Flock of Seagulls	"Space Age Love Song"	PHOTOGRAPHY: Elizabeth Baptiste
		DESIGN: Maude Gilman
		1982, Jive 2003, U.S.

Synth-pop groups Thompson Twins and A Flock of Seagulls benefited during the early, fledgling days of MTV, when few artists had music videos. They rocketed to stardom as a result of their continuous exposure.

Pre-*Edward Scissorhands*, Flock's lead singer (and former hairdresser) Mike Score drew additional attention to the band with his curiously abstract hairstyles.

The Thompson Twins rivaled with their own intricate hair designs, immortalized in the Thompson Twins' logo (shown in the upper left corner of the "Doctor! Doctor!" sleeve).

Thompson Twins designer Andie Airfix: "I worked primarily with member Alannah [Currie], and she was incredibly creative and aware of the balance between commercialism without diluting it with visuals. We would work on designs and then present them to the band. They recognized that we had a strong creative relationship and usually went with the directions we chose. This was usually a combination of great photos and stylistic bold graphics that complimented their logo—their 'branding'—a horrible word, but in essence what made their sleeves instantly recognizable."

Bronski Beat + Marc Almond	"I Feel Love"	DESIGN: Gill Whisson
		1985, Forbidden Fruit / Bite 4, U.K.

Dance club staples Bronski Beat and Book of Love brought out their inner child for "I Feel Love" and "Witchcraft."

Former Bronski Beat lead Jimmy Somerville: "The cover [for 'I Feel Love'] was a '50s-inspired piece of kitsch. It had a childish, innocent look, but we were anything but!"

One of the first openly gay pop artists, Somerville explains that the single "caused all sorts of grief, the main being, yes, you guessed it, the homo connotations." Long before *Brokeback Mountain*, his "I Feel Love" medley winked at romance on the range by including "Johnny Remember Me," a cowboy song from the '60s. The back of the sleeve additionally featured a vintage Bonanza postcard, which spurred legal issues.

Book of Love

"Witchcraft"

PLAY-DOH: **Lauren Johnson**
ART DIRECTION: **Jade Lee**
1989, Warner Bros. 21251 {12"}, U.S.

Book of Love's "Witchcraft" jacket, which was crafted from Play-Doh, was similarly tongue-in-cheek. Member Lauren Johnson: "Wow, was always hoping to be recognized for my Play-Doh skills. Finally! I originally wanted to do it with Jell-O."

"Witchcraft" was a nod to the '60s sitcom *Bewitched*. "The band has always been into TV and pop culture," explains Johnson. "We were big into sampling and loved all the sound effects they used on *Bewitched* (i.e., when Samantha said an incantation to cast a spell, or wiggled her nose, or the sound effect when a spell went wrong). Ted [Ottaviano] made up this crazy narrative based on casting spells and tragic love stories from Greek mythology, mixed with names of herbs used to make love potions. The final twist was having the choruses be the names of Samantha's witch relatives Aunt Hagatha, Aunt Clara, and Endora. The song was also a bow to The B-52's '52 Girls.'"

| Poison | "I Want Action" | DESIGN: Unknown
1986, Enigma 44004, U.S. |

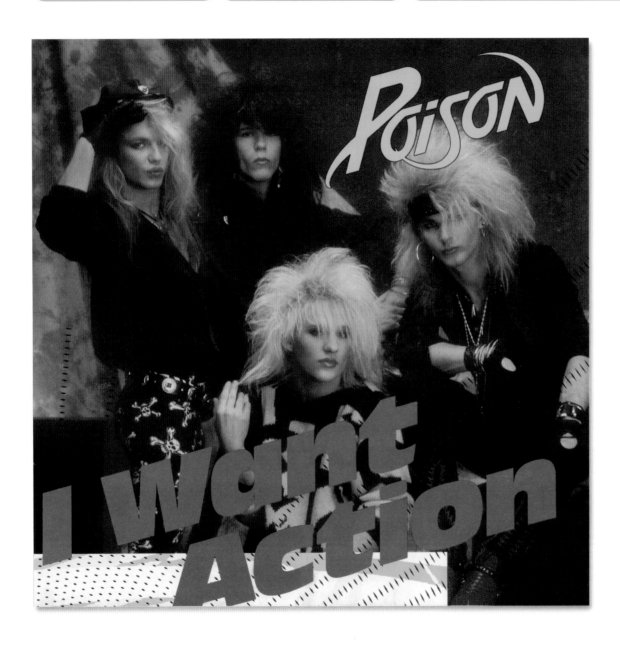

| Mötley Crüe | "Smokin' in the Boys Room" | DESIGN: Unknown
1985, Elektra 966864-0 {12"}, U.K. |

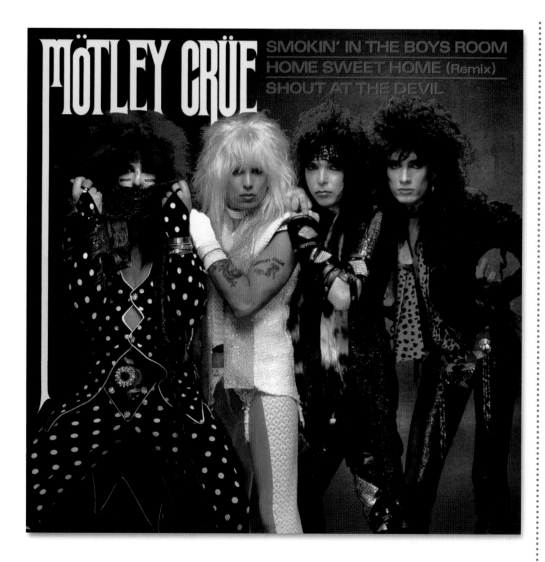

MÖTLEY CRÜE
SMOKIN' IN THE BOYS ROOM
HOME SWEET HOME (Remix)
SHOUT AT THE DEVIL

Glam metal bands Poison and Mötley Crüe forged the blueprint for mid-'80s excess and hair band wannabes.

Aqua Net, check.

Extreme makeup, check.

Wild apparel, check.

The themes of their singles synced perfectly with their raucous images, from Poison's "I Want Action" and "Talk Dirty to Me" to Mötley Crüe's "Smokin' in the Boys Room" and "Girls, Girls, Girls."

| a-ha | "Train of Thought" | ILLUSTRATION: | Michael Patterson / Candace Reckinger 1986, Warner 8736, U.K. |

a-ha's groundbreaking video, *Take on Me* (1985), blended live action with hand-drawn animation. One of the sketches was used for their "Train of Thought" sleeve (shown here).

Animator Mike Patterson describes how his student film *Commuter* led to a-ha and the *Take on Me* clip: "I wanted to develop a style that could capture the fleeting moments of life in a very animated and vibrant way. My film [*Commuter*] was being broadcast in Europe and in the U.S.; a producer saw it and brought the piece to Warner Records, who were adamant about not deviating from the movement and drawing style used in the film. My wife Candace Reckinger and I had begun working as a team, and this was our first big project."

"[*Take on Me*] took about sixteen weeks in our small studio, and I did every single drawing. I think that's why the piece flows so nicely. Candace designed the opening to the clip to have the feel of Japanese action comics at the time."

"I never imagined [how well the video would be received]. I love the fact that kids who were born ten years after it was made have seen it, and love it. That's fantastic, and something only pop culture can do."

Take on Me went on to win six MTV Video Music Awards, and Patterson's *Commuter* landed in MoMA (The Museum of Modern Art). Patterson followed with other innovative projects, including Paula Abdul's *Opposites Attract* video (which earned him a Grammy). He has since moved onto commercial advertising, films, and education.

| Chaka Khan | "I Feel for You" | ILLUSTRATION: Anne Field
ART DIRECTION: Simon Levy
DESIGN: Kav DeLuxe
1984, Warner 29195, U.S. |

Chaka Khan's "I Feel for You" featured a similar, hand-sketched aesthetic on the cover. The single was originally recorded by Prince on his debut album. Khan's version featured guest rapper Melle Mel and Stevie Wonder on harmonica.

Run-D.M.C.	"Mary, Mary"	PHOTOGRAPHY: Janette Beckman
		DESIGN: Marlene Cohen
		1988, Profile 5211, U.S.

Run-D.M.C. brought hip-hop to the mainstream.

While Run-D.M.C. was breaking ground at radio with their hard-hitting lyrics and fusion of rap and rock, they defined street style with their baggy clothing, rope chains, and Adidas shoes (laces removed, of course). From left to right on the "Mary, Mary" sleeve: Darryl "D.M.C." McDaniels, Jason "Jam Master Jay" Mizell, and Joseph "Run" Simmons.

McDaniels: "The Adidas song came about when a guy named Dr. Dees put out an editorial called *Felon Shoes*, which kind of 'judged a book by its cover' for all the neighborhood youth. Yes, it's true that drug dealers and Stick-Up Kids wore Adidas, gold chains, Kangols, and Lees/Levis, but so did the college kids and hard working youth who didn't seek the 'fast life.' We wrote it to let the world know that these sneakers do more than just stand on corners. They travel the world doing positive things, too."

While other rappers typically rapped over disco, R&B, and funk records, Run-D.M.C. dusted off the rock LPs. "Disco always had a bass line for the MC to run his mouth. James Brown always had a funky drummer beat. Funk and R&B always had a break, but in the DJ crates were also the rock albums," says McDaniels.

They landed in the U.S. Rock & Roll Hall of Fame in 2008 as a result, the second rap group to be inducted. "I am, and always will be a Rock & Roll head. I love The Beatles, Led Zeppelin, Janis Joplin, Dylan, The Stones, Fogerty, Neil Young, CSN+Y, Hendrix, etc.," explains McDaniels, "but it doesn't get any better than Lennon and Sarah McLachlan," whom McDaniels says have inspired him the most. "Peace, Love, Hip-Hop, and Rock & Roll!"

| Iron Maiden | "The Trooper" | PAINTING: Derek Riggs
1983, EMI 5397, U.K. |

Metallica	"One"	ILLUSTRATION: **Pushead**
		DESIGN: Reiner Design Consultants, Inc.
		1988, Elektra 69329, U.S.

Perhaps the two most influential heavy metal bands of the '80s, Britain's Iron Maiden and America's Metallica frequently used cryptic cover art.

"The Trooper" (featuring cover art regular "Eddie" the skeleton) references the Crimean War, while "One" is based on the novel *Johnny Got His Gun* by Dalton Trumbo (about a soldier wounded in World War I).

Longtime Iron Maiden artist Derek Riggs details the saga behind *The Trooper* sleeve: "I got the call from Maiden, as usual, on a Thursday night. They wanted the artwork by Monday morning. This left me Friday to rush out to the shops and get some reference material for the uniform."

"The song was about the Charge of the Light Brigade, which was a nasty military defeat in which they [British cavalry] charged the Russians and got slaughtered. I originally had more dead Russians in the sketch, but due to the horrible time constraints I had to leave most of them out, so there are just a couple of hands and a cannon."

"I worked over the weekend without sleep to get the artwork finished on time. I used to deliver the paintings to Maiden's office by taxi cab, and when the cab arrived [for 'The Trooper'] I was still painting the picture, adding the little details, etc. I finished this off quickly and the painting had to dry on the way to Maiden's office. I even had the taxi window open so that the wind would speed up the drying paint."

"When I got to the office I found out that they didn't really need it until Wednesday, so I could have had a few days more to paint it...or at least get some sleep."

"This was a common way of working when doing Maiden's covers. Some people wonder why I stopped doing them."

| Berlin | "The Metro" | PHOTOGRAPHY: Ed Colver
1983, Geffen 29638, U.S. |

"The Metro" and "Gone Daddy Gone" had Berlin and the Violent Femmes searching for love lost.

Berlin's Terri Nunn: "John [Crawford, founding member] wrote 'The Metro' about a girlfriend who was going to Europe at the time. He was afraid that she would meet a dashing European guy and dump him."

Nunn continues, "Berlin started in '79, and it was a couple of years of writing and playing before identifying ourselves. We knew we wanted to be electronic, like Kraftwerk and Ultravox in England, and there wasn't really anything like that in America. We wanted to bring that over here and put our stamp on it; having a female vocal with that kind of music was unique."

"When we finished 'The Metro,' we thought 'This is it. This is what Berlin is, and that's what we're going to fashion all of the other songs around.' It ranks as one of my all-time favorites, still."

Regarding "The Metro's" sleeve, "I love that photo! Such a great cover," says Nunn. "It was taken at an awful, downtown, broken down area in California. They put fragile, waif-looking me in the area and shot around all this graffiti, ruins, broken glass, and hypodermic needles."

Violent Femmes	"Gone Daddy Gone"	PHOTOGRAPHY: Ron Hugo
		DESIGN: Jeff Price
		1983, Slash 882001-1 {12"}, U.K.

The Violent Femmes' sleeve featured 3-year-old Billie Jo Campbell, who was randomly selected on the streets of L.A. as she was walking with her mother. Campbell was paid $100 for the shoot, and told to look in the door of an old house to see a living room full of animals. She didn't find them, and became irritated by the time this particular photograph was taken. Decades later, Campbell is still recognized for the famous shot.

Stray Cats	"(She's) Sexy + 17"	ILLUSTRATION: Ed "Big Daddy" Roth
		DESIGN: Henry Marquez
		1983, EMI America 8168, U.S.

The Stray Cats brought rockabilly back to radio with hits including "Rock this Town" and "Stray Cat Strut," while the Ramones led the punk rock movement into the '80s with "Baby, I Love You" and "The KKK Took My Baby Away," among other tracks. Both bands also pulled underground cartoonists into the limelight.

Stray Cats' drummer Slim Jim Phantom discusses the selection of Ed "Big Daddy" Roth (creator of hot-rod icon Rat Fink) for their artwork: "We were very interested in tracking down classic people and things we admired. Ed Roth was certainly one of them. We just had a big hit in the States, so the label was accommodating."

"We met Roth in a hotel in San Francisco. He had great ideas right away and did some stuff right there. Roth had been asked by quite a few bands to do artwork for them, but turned everybody down. Apparently, he was religious and didn't want to work with anyone whose music he considered unholy. He liked us and the music."

"We used his artwork for a bunch of stuff— tour posters, other single sleeves, etc. [It was] one of those rare, impetuous moves that you make when you're young that are now seen as strokes of genius. We just loved his work in the old hot rod mags."

RAMONES

Rock 'N' Roll HIGH SCHOOL

Rock 'N' Roll High School

GABBA GABBA HEY!

T.N.T.

WBN 17.568

Similarly, the Ramones helped bring illustrator William Stout's comic style to the mainstream with "Rock 'N' Roll High School." Originally a contributor for *Bomp!* and *Heavy Metal* magazines, Stout eventually moved beyond illustrations and into other areas of design, including Disney theme parks, ZZ Top's Recycler tour, and even Michael Jackson's Neverland Ranch.

| Devo | "Working in a Coalmine" | PHOTOGRAPHY: Shakey Pictures (film still from *Human Highway*) 1981, Virgin / VS 457, U.K. |

In 1978, Devo's Mark Mothersbaugh tagged Akron, Ohio "the second Liverpool." While he was referring to the grayness of the industrial city's skies, his phrase was interpreted by the press as meaning that Akron was a hotbed for '80s talent.

It was.

In the late '70s and early '80s, record executives scoured the city for "the Akron sound," coming up with the likes of Devo, Chrissie Hynde of the Pretenders, and The Waitresses, among others.

Devo's Gerald Casale: "Growing up in Akron, Ohio, and being raised blue collar made it easy to identify with songs such as Lee Dorsey's 'Workin' in a Coalmine.' Blues and R&B filled the AM and FM airwaves broadcast out of Cleveland, Detroit, and Chicago. It was my favorite music."

"When I landed an honors college work/study scholarship at Kent State University I floated out of my depressed and politically charged Akron/Cleveland reality for a short while embracing psychedelia in all its forms. Still, I was playing in a blues band and I joined SDS [Student for a Democratic Society]."

"I admitted Allison Krause and Jeffery Miller to Kent State, advising them on their freshman curriculum as part of my summer work program at the University. Nine months later I was a short distance away from them when they were both shot dead as we all ran from the National Guard, choking on tear gas fumes."

"I died in my own way that day and was reborn—no more Mr. Nice Guy. I started formulating the philosophy of De-evolution and met Mark Mothersbaugh all in short order."

"The rest is history."

651315 7

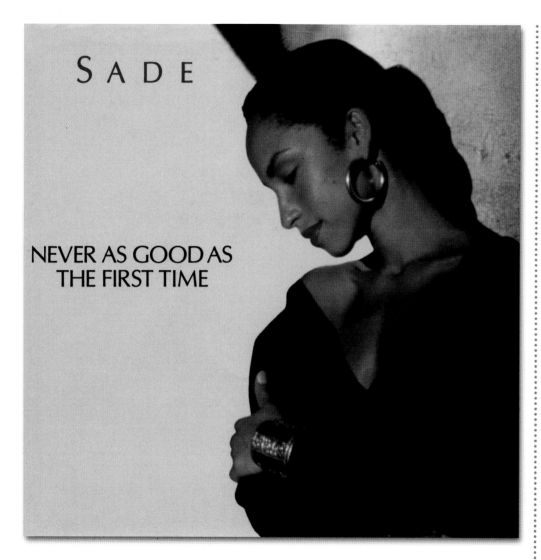

SADE

NEVER AS GOOD AS
THE FIRST TIME

Both here in reflective poses, Terence Trent D'Arby and Sade uniquely mixed soul, rock, pop, R&B, and jazz in their music.

D'Arby adopted the name Sananda Maitreya in 2001.

Maitreya on "Sign Your Name": "I recall in 1985, after seeing *Live Aid* on television (I was living in Frankfurt, Germany, at the time), falling asleep that night and dreaming of Sade, for whom I had a little crush, asking me to write her a song."

"I remember her performance of 'Is It a Crime' knocking me out. Thereafter a few days later I remember coming up with 'Sign Your Name' and knowing that it was in response to Sade's dream request."

"Needless to say, I kept the song for myself. If you listen to 'Sign Your Name' you might be able to tell that it was written according to her particular style at the time, but it also betrays my love for one of my favourite musician/composers of all time, the genius Brazilian, Antonio Carlos Jobim."

"I had occasion to meet Maestra [Sade] Adu, about a year later, and gushingly announced to her that I would be as big as she and that I was a great fan. Time has only raised my appreciation for her oeuvre."

"A post note: I subsequently wrote 'Delicate' for the both of us only to be rebuffed by Sony and assigned another artist [Des'ree]."

"I am not sure that history would give Sade credit for being a huge influence on that particular time in TTD's life and career. The usual rock and R&B suspects are mentioned, but she should be added firmly to his list of influences. God bless her!"

Best known for collaborating on a series of '80s club anthems (e.g., Pet Shop Boys' "West End Girls," Divine's "Shoot Your Shot"), writer/producer Bobby O recorded "I Cry for You" as a solo single. The twelve-inch sleeve was adapted from pop artist Roy Lichtenstein's 1963 piece *In the Car*.

Lichtenstein's venture into pop art followed a challenge by one of his sons in the early '60s, who pointed to a Mickey Mouse comic book and said "I bet you can't paint as good as that!" Lichtenstein took up the dare and began making cartoon images. He used an industrial approach for many of his works, painting with exaggerated Ben-day dots [tiny, colored dots used in '50s and '60s pulp comic books to create shading].

West London band, The Flames, used a similar comic-style for their single, "Your Love Is Slippin' Away."

Tina Turner

"Steamy Windows"

PHOTOGRAPHY: **Herb Ritts**
DESIGN: **Glenn Sakamoto**
1989, Capitol 44473, U.S.

TINA TURNER STEAMY WINDOWS

Following her split from Ike Turner, Tina Turner's status as an entertainer waned until collaborating with former members of The Human League, Ian Craig Marsh and Martyn Ware. Their version of the Temptations' "Ball of Confusion" caught the eye of Capitol Records, who later signed Tina as a solo artist and released her comeback LP *Private Dancer*.

Choreographer Toni Basil was also brought in during this period. "They contacted me when Tina left Ike, and I have worked with her throughout the years," says Basil. "Tina is so high energy—a workaholic! She is also one of the few iconic stars that get applause when they perform certain dance steps. "Proud Mary" is a perfect example. People wait patiently for those classic moves." Basil choreographed several of Tina's tours, including her 2008/2009 50th Anniversary trek (which opened with Tina's rock anthem "Steamy Windows," shown here).

Aside from Tina, Basil has choreographed several other pop icons, including David Bowie and Bette Midler. However, her "work with David Byrne—particularly 'Once in a Lifetime,' is what Basil considers her most memorable and innovative collaboration, which had Bryne moving as a marionette.

TONI BASIL
MICKEY

Photographer: Sherry Rayn Barnett

Basil had an international smash of her own with "Mickey." "The cheerleading theme came from my experience as a head cheerleader," explains Basil, "the stomping and cheering in a basketball court was always wonderful, and it echoed so well, so I thought it might sound great for the video and single. My record company, of course, begged me not to do this idea."

| Yazoo | "Only You" | DESIGN: Rocking Rick Lego
1982, Mute 020, U.K. |

Vince Clarke initially offered his torch song "Only You" to Depeche Mode before leaving the band in 1981. He subsequently formed Yazoo (or just "Yaz" in the States) with bluesy vocalist Alison Moyet, and "Only You" became the group's first hit (U.K. #2.)

Yazoo scored again on the charts with songs including "Don't Go," "Situation," and "The Other Side of Love" before folding in 1983. Moyet established a successful solo career while Clarke moved to Erasure.

Modern English	"Gathering Dust"	DESIGN: **23 Envelope**
		1980, 4AD 15, U.K.

GATHERING DUST

"Only You's" football sketch shared similar design characteristics with "Gathering Dust." Modern English (best known for "I Melt with You"), based "Dust's" sleeve on the Diane Arbus photograph *Retired Man and His Wife at Home in a Nudist Camp One Morning* (1963).

Modern English lead Robbie Grey: "Artwork was very important for us. I remember Ivo [Watts-Russell] at 4AD had a Diane Arbus book that we looked through. We saw the picture of the naked couple and liked the feeling of isolation they had with the room. The TV set caught our eye because at the early Modern English concerts we had a TV set on stage with the name of the band across the screen. Also, if you look closely you will see a few birds flying on the cover. That relates to the b-side, 'Tranquility of a Summer Moment (Vice Versa).'"

| Erasure | "Victim of Love" | DESIGN: Paul White @ Me Co. |
| | | 1987, Mute 61, U.K. |

| The Sugarcubes | "Deus" | DESIGN: Paul White @ Me Co. |
| | | 1988, One Little Indian / 10TP10 {10"}, U.K. |

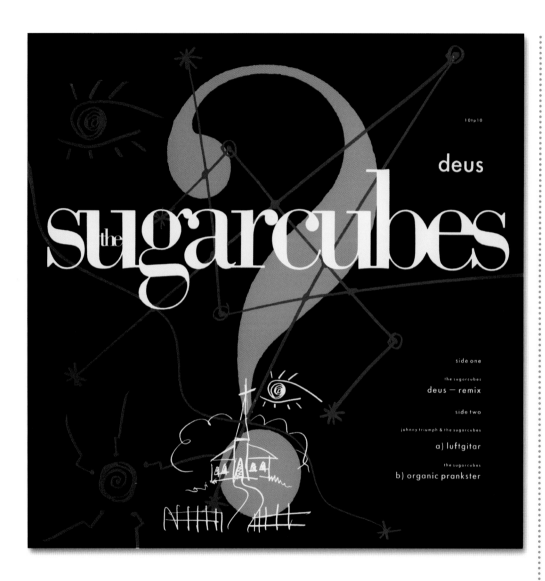

Erasure and The Sugarcubes (fronted by Björk) were two of the only groups in the '80s that consistently refrained from using self-portraits as sleeve art.

"This was purely down to vanity in some cases," quips Erasure's Andy Bell. "I think it is more vain *not to have* a photo on the sleeve, because you're saying 'you can't look at me.'"

Bell describes the thought process behind "Victim of Love": "The first album, *Wonderland*, was based on a collection of fairytale books that I had as a child, and represented innocence and the loss of innocence. I just love unrequited love, and I suppose that this crosses over into our single/album cover artwork—lots of bloody hearts. [It is also] based on those psychoanalytic ink drawings."

"[With our sleeve art] usually we get together and have a bit of an afternoon brainstorming, joking, and fantasizing. We come up with a feeling more than anything else. The singles always seem to flow naturally from the album artwork just by deciding on key colors or by zooming in and out of the originals, exploring them in some way."

Both "Victim of Love" and "Deus" were designed by Paul White at Me Company. "I enjoyed my meetings with Paul at the time, 'cause he's very handsome and I fancied him," jokes Bell.

Despite the lack of face time on their cover artwork, Andy Bell and Vince Clark are front and center during live performances, converting even the most intimate of club shows into dazzling spectacles. "I just love the idea of true theatre," explains Bell, "creating a visual and enchanting experience out of nothing but maybe paper and shadows, darkness and light."

| The Smiths | "What Difference Does It Make?" | PHOTOGRAPHY: Columbia Pictures
DESIGN: Morrissey
1984, Rough Trade 146, U.K. |

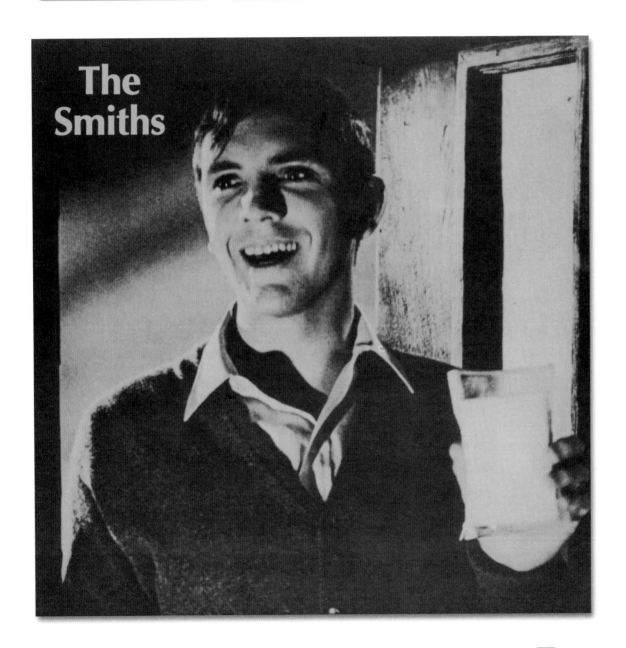

The Smiths	"What Difference Does It Make?"	PHOTOGRAPHY:	Neil Phillips
		DESIGN:	Morrissey
			1984, Rough Trade 146, U.K.

The Smiths

The initial release for The Smiths' coincidentally titled "What Difference Does It Make?" contained a still of actor Terence Stamp from the 1965 film *The Collector*.

When Stamp objected to the use of his image, Morrissey reshot the cover and lampooned Stamp's exact pose, mockingly holding a glass of milk instead of a chloroform pad.

Stamp eventually gave permission and the original cover was reinstated.

"She Works Hard for the Money"

PHOTOGRAPHY: Harry Langdon
DESIGN: Chris Whorf @ Art Hotel
1983, Mercury 812370, U.S.

Dolly Parton	"9 to 5"	PHOTOGRAPHY: Ron Slenzak ART DIRECTION: George Corsillo / Tim Bryant @ Gribbit 1980, RCA 12133, U.S. {backside of 7" sleeve}

Mothers went back to work in the '80s.

Films such as Mr. Mom and *Baby Boom*, television shows like *Cagney and Lacey* and *Alice*, and songs, including Donna Summer's "She Works Hard for the Money" and Dolly Parton's "9 to 5" all reflected the trials and tribulations of the "working girl."

Stateside, "9 to 5" was revisited several times. It was a hit song and feature film in 1980, a television series from '82–'83 and '86–'88, and a Broadway show nearly thirty years later (in 2009).

| Samantha Fox | "Touch Me (I Want Your Body)" | DESIGN: | Unknown |
| | | | 1986, Jive 1006, U.S. |

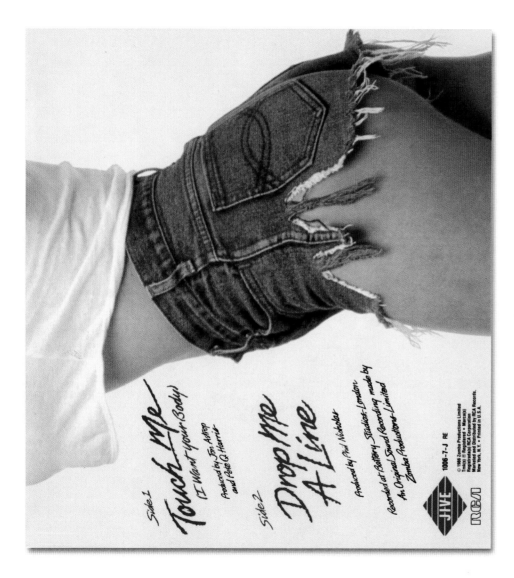

The most photographed women in Britain during the 1980s were Margaret Thatcher, Princess Diana...and Samantha Fox.

At age 16, Samantha Fox posed topless and became a "Page Three Girl" in the U.K. newspaper *The Sun*. Editions containing Fox's photos flew off the newsstands. She went on to win "Page Three Girl of the Year" honors for three consecutive years.

In 1986, she moved beyond the layouts and decided to give singing a shot.

Enlisting an impressive roster of producers, including Stock Aitken Waterman (Dead or Alive, Bananarama) and Full Force (Lisa Lisa and Cult Jam), Fox scored again.

Fox: "I was a singer/performer before I became a model. I even had a band at age 15. At the height of my modeling career, I was offered many songs to record. When I heard 'Touch Me,' I knew this was the one."

Debut single "Touch Me (I Want Your Body)" was available as a foldout single in the U.S., giving the impression of a magazine centerfold. However, "in England it was just a head shot as I wanted to be accepted as a serious musician," says Fox.

Other U.S. Top 10 hits included "Naughty Girls (Need Love Too)" and "I Wanna Have Some Fun," while the U.K. put "Do Ya Do Ya (Wanna Please Me)" and "Nothing's Gonna Stop Me Now" in their Top 10.

BLANCMANGE

"Blind Vision"

Blank Vinyl Version

Retro kitsch from synthpop's Blancmange and prog rock's It Bites.

Blancmange's Neil Arthur on "Blind Vision": "The sleeve idea is taken from a Symington's Table Cream poster, although showing the woman holding the single sleeve instead of the originally advertised product."

As was typical with most Blancmange sleeves, the group's namesake was visually symbolized (see the pink dessert).

"Our name was chosen at a party Stephen Luscombe threw," says Arthur. "I had gone out and bought an Indian curry dish and on returning to the party dropped it on the floor. I scooped the food into a pint drinking glass and Stephen came along with a blancmange rabbit on a plate. He asked, 'so what are we going to call ourselves?' and we looked at the immediate choices, the blancmange verses a pint of curry. 'The Blancmange' won. We later dropped the 'The.' At the time there were so many bands with long names, like The Bleak Industrial Cooling Towers, etc. We wanted to get on with the music, rather than exhaust ourselves with a name. Although, on reflection... it could have been 'A Pint Of Curry.'"

It Bites

"Calling All the Heroes"

ILLUSTRATION: **Viv Mabon**
ART DIRECTION: **It Bites**
DESIGN: **Stylorouge**
1986, Virgin / VS 872, U.K.

Regarding It Bites' nostalgic cover for "Calling All The Heroes," drummer Bob Dalton explains that "the idea came from [keyboardist] John Beck, who also came up with the concept for the first album cover [*The Big Lad in the Windmill*]. Once we had a concept, we would sit around and develop it as far as we could with crude artwork, then pass it to the art department."

However, hit singles and slick artwork weren't a prime focus of the band. Despite industry pressure to duplicate the success of "Calling All the Heroes," "we never wanted to make the same album for the sake of trying to make money. The music was always first and success, if it came, was always secondary," says Dalton.

produced by chris butler

The cult '80s flick *The Last American Virgin* featured a memorable scene (backed by "I Know What Boys Like"), in which the male lead picks up three girls with the promise of cocaine. They instead had powdered sugar, which the girls proclaimed as "the best Colombian they ever had!"

The scene mirrored the experiences of The Waitresses' front man Chris Butler.

"I was living in the Highland Square area of Akron, Ohio," says Butler, "which was Hipsterville in Akron (and still a great area). There was a bar called The Bucket Shop, a major watering hole. I would go and see all these women getting picked up by lawyers and stockbrokers who had mountains of blow. I was sorta' cool, was in a great, signed rock band…and couldn't get laid. So the song is about the teasing that went on there, night after night, and my crankiness in going home alone."

The photo on the sleeve was a junior high school yearbook shot of ZE Records' Andy Furman. "It just looked so sweet and innocent," says Butler, "seemed perfect."

The song lives on. "I have been contacted by a number of strippers over the years that tell me that they have built their acts around this song," quips Butler. "But, I guess when I see a commercial t-shirt on a cute girl, or a gay guy—that's the best, because the phrase has endured and become a part of the culture."

Marilyn

"You Don't Love Me"

PHOTOGRAPHY: Johnny Rozsa
DESIGN: Da Gama
1984, Love / MAZ 3, U.K.

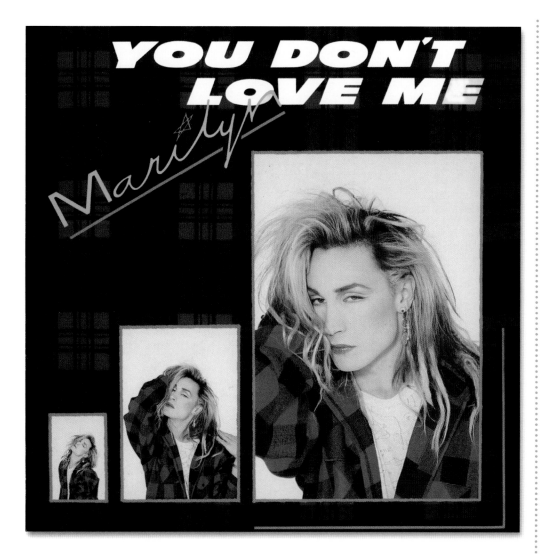

Gender-bending pop star Marilyn similarly voiced pent-up frustrations in "You Don't Love Me." An off-and-on pal with Boy George, Marilyn first gained attention in Eurythmics' *Who's That Girl?* video. He later hit #4 in the U.K. (and #1 in Japan) with "Calling Your Name."

| Buggles | "Clean Clean" | DESIGN: Glenn Travis Associates
1980, Island / WIP 6584, U.K. |

GENERALS AND MAJORS

Housed in tongue-in-cheek sleeves, new wave gems "Clean Clean" and "Generals and Majors" continued the stream of '80s singles that were focused on war and peace. Lively dance floor beats masked the songs' sobering lyrics.

"Clean Clean" was "loosely inspired on one side by the comedy of *M*A*S*H*, and on the other by the tragedy of the Vietnam War (the lyric 'lost a million in our very first attack')," says Geoff Downes of the Buggles.

Downes continues, "'Clean Clean' was an odd cover, to say the least; a comic book shooting gallery of me, Trevor [Horn], and an unknown soldier. However, there was no major outcry to the [seemingly controversial] sleeve. I guess people thought we were just a pair of crackpot studio musicians having a laugh. They let us do our thing. Much of our style was tragic-comic."

Public Enemy	"Bring the Noise"	PHOTOGRAPHY: Andrew Catlin
		1987, Def Jam 651335, U.K.

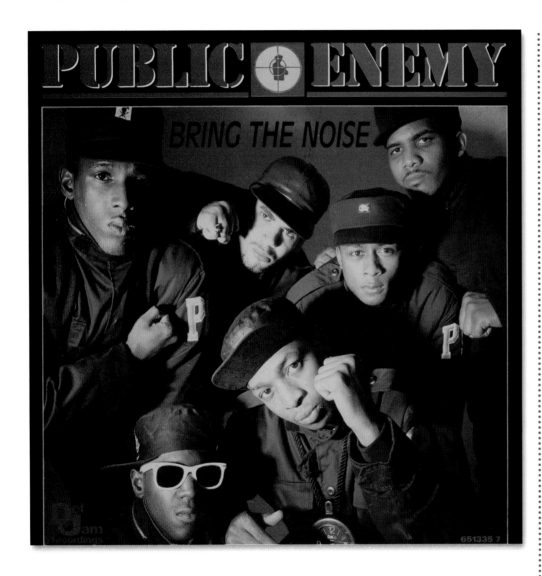

Rick Rubin, legendary producer and co-founder of Def Jam Recordings, was instrumental in jump-starting the careers of Public Enemy and the Beastie Boys.

Politically-charged Public Enemy was discovered by Rubin when he heard PE frontman Chuck D, rapping on a demo. Public Enemy's '80s albums *Yo! Bum Rush the Show* and *It Takes a Nation of Millions to Hold Us Back* progressed rap into a more political, socially conscious direction.

Beastie Boys	"No Sleep Till Brooklyn"	PHOTOGRAPHY: Glen E. Friedman
		DESIGN: Eric Haze
		1987, Def Jam 06675, U.S.

Initially a punk band, the Beastie Boys became the first successful white rap group when they joined forces with Rubin in 1984. After being tapped by Madonna to open her Virgin Tour and by Run-D.M.C. for their Raising Hell trek, the Beastie Boys released *Licensed to III* (produced by Rubin). It was an immediate success.

| Olivia Newton-John | "Twist of Fate" | PHOTOGRAPHY: Herb Ritts
ART DIRECTION: George Osaki
DESIGN: Norman Moore
1983, MCA 52284, U.S. |

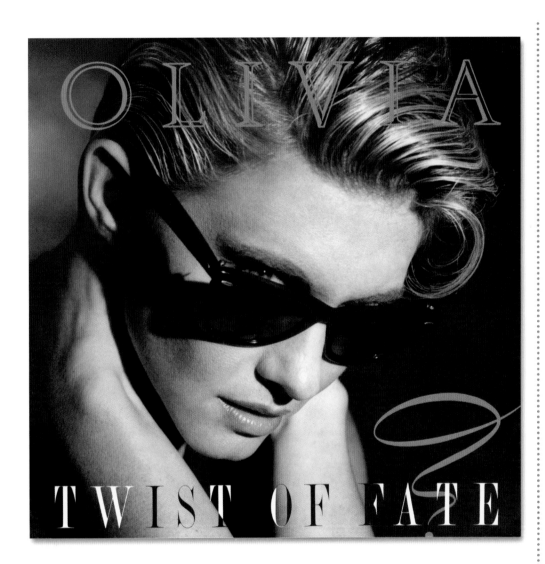

Notable music photographers Herb Ritts (Madonna, Tina Turner) and Richard Haughton (Siousxie Sioux, Duran Duran) capture Olivia Newton-John and Everything But The Girl in black-and-white stunners.

"Twist of Fate" headed the soundtrack for the film *Two of a Kind*, which reunited *Grease* co-stars Olivia Newton-John and John Travolta. The single followed a series of '80s hits for Newton-John, which included "Magic," "Xanadu," and "Physical."

Everything But the Girl	"Don't Leave Me Behind"	PHOTOGRAPHY: Richard Haughton
		DESIGN: Caryn Gough
		1986, Blanco Y Negro 23, U.K.

Everything But The Girl

"Don't Leave Me Behind" was an early pop hit from Everything But the Girl, who changed musical direction to a more electronic sound following their massively successful '95 single, "Missing."

Madonna and Prince crossed over to the big screen with their critically and commercially successful films *Desperately Seeking Susan* and *Purple Rain*. The classic sleeve images also doubled as movie poster artwork.

Herb Ritts shot the sleeve for "Into the Groove." Ritts went on to form a long-standing friendship with Madonna, lensing her *True Blue*, *Like a Prayer*, and *Immaculate Collection* LP artwork, among other projects.

"The Ritts image [shown here] was 100% Madonna's styling," says *Desperately Seeking Susan* publicist Reid Rosefelt, but "Madonna hated the jacket. It was [production/costume designer] Santo Loquasto's idea, not hers. It was 'thrift store' and Madonna had a very distinct image, which was the teddy, the 'Boy Toy' belt, the cross and other big necklaces, the plastic bangles. She brought as much of that stuff as she could into the movie, and very definitely into this poster/ single cover, as Santo wasn't there."

This iconic shot wasn't the studio's original idea for the poster, says Rosefelt. "Sometime after the film wrapped, I happened to be at the Orion [movie studio] office in New York for a publicity meeting when the ad agency was making a presentation. The focus was on the New Jersey housewife part of the movie. Rosanna [Arquette]'s face was on a toaster and Madonna's face was on a piece of toast. Also, [another concept] with a microwave oven. Each one was more terrible than the one before. As it happened, I had bought a set of the slides from the Ritts photo session to the meeting. I pulled them out and said, 'have you guys seen these?' They hadn't. There was a hush in the room."

"This wasn't the end of the story," however, continues Rosefelt. "Some people at Orion thought that the image would make people think it was a lesbian movie. Thankfully the film's producers, Midge Sanford and Sarah Pillsbury, were able to make their case and the result is the image that you see here."

Prince and The Revolution

"Let's Go Crazy"

PHOTOGRAPHY: **Ed Thrasher & Associates**
ART DIRECTOR: **Prince**
DESIGN: **Laura LiPuma-Nash**
1984, Warner 29216, U.S.

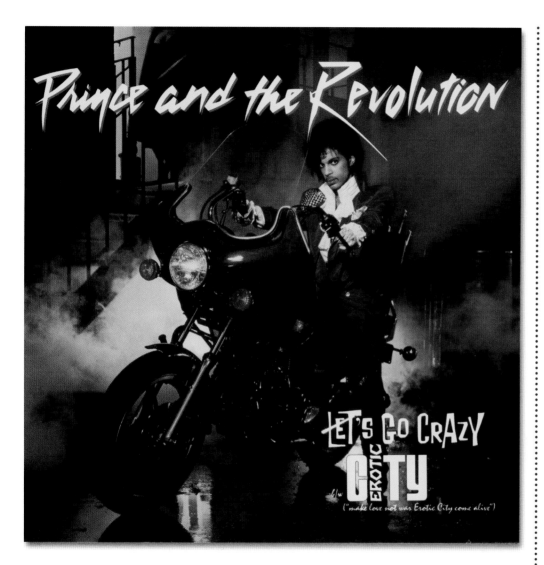

Laura LiPuma-Nash was Prince's designer at Warner Bros. for much of the '80s (including the "Let's Go Crazy" single, shown here), and describes her initial meeting with Prince:

"Warner Bros. hired me in 1982 as a staff graphic designer/art director. Within my first couple months I happened to be the only one in the art department during the lunch hour one day, when a call from Prince came in requesting to see an art director ASAP about a single sleeve design. So, off I went to meet with Prince, and that was the beginning of a five-year run as Prince's exclusive in-house art director at WB. Considering how young I was and the short amount of time I had been on staff, it took all the confidence I would muster to get through the challenge of working with such an intimidating superstar. Prince is extremely methodical and has a specific plan for everything."

Entrepreneur Jay King beat the music industry odds when he independently pressed and promoted Timex Social Club's 12" smash "Rumors."

"We sent the single to radio with my home phone number on the back of the sleeve," says King. "KKDA in Dallas featured it on their 'Make It or Break It' challenge and the phone calls were through the roof. The station rang me and asked that I stop telling my family and friends to call for the song." When King informed the station that he lived in California he knew that he had a potential hit on his hands. Timex Social Club went on to sell 6.5 million units worldwide.

"Rumors" even generated its own rumors, with the public curious as to who "Michael," "Tina," and "Susan" were in the lyrics. "We were referencing Michael Jackson, Tina Turner, and Susan Anton, although at the time we sometimes said Susan Moonsie from Vanity 6," says King.

Club Nouveau	"Lean on Me"	ILLUSTRATION: Mary Kelleher Smith
		DESIGN: Steven Migli
		1987, King Jay / Tommy Boy 894 {12"}, U.S

Following the success of "Rumors," King signed with Warner Brothers, forming King Jay Records and the R&B collective Club Nouveau. Their cover of Bill Withers' "Lean on Me" hit #1 in the states and #3 in the U.K.

The 80s airbrushed style of the "Rumors" single continued on with four consecutive Club Nouveau singles: "Jealousy," "Situation #9," "Lean on Me," and "Why You Treat Me So Bad." King set out to "create a character and continue a visual story" with each of the singles.

| Talk Talk | "It's My Life" | ILLUSTRATION: James Marsh |
| | | 1984, EMI America 8195, U.S. |

B-8195

| Squeeze | "Tempted" | ILLUSTRATION: **Patricia Dryden**
ART DIRECTION: **Jeff Ayeroff**
DESIGN: **Melanie Nissen**
1981, A&M 2345, U.S. |

"It's My Life" and "Tempted" had similarly structured contemporary art covers.

Conceptual artist and designer James Marsh based the sleeve art for "It's My Life" on one of his paintings. *"It's My Life* was an existing piece that happened to fit the title," explains Marsh. "The single was a sliced portion cropped from that painting, and the idea of the puzzle pieces coming together to form a whole picture of life is straightforward symbolism. The pieces also incorporated two vital parts of [John Everett] Millais' painting *The Boyhood Of Raleigh* (1871), which portrays a boy learning about life at sea."

Marsh designed nearly every Talk Talk album and single sleeve that was released. "I'm still a fan of Talk Talk," says Marsh, "good work always holds up over time."

"Tempted" was illustrated by Patricia Dryden. The single featured vocals by Paul Carrack ("Don't Shed a Tear") and Elvis Costello.

Billy Idol	"Rebel Yell"	PHOTOGRAPHY: Albert Sanchez
		1985, Chrysalis / Idol 6, U.K.

PHOTOGRAPHY:	Raúl Vega
ART DIRECTION:	Henry Marquez
DESIGN:	Michael Diehl
	1984, EMI America 8203, U.S.

Corey Hart

"Sunglasses at Night"

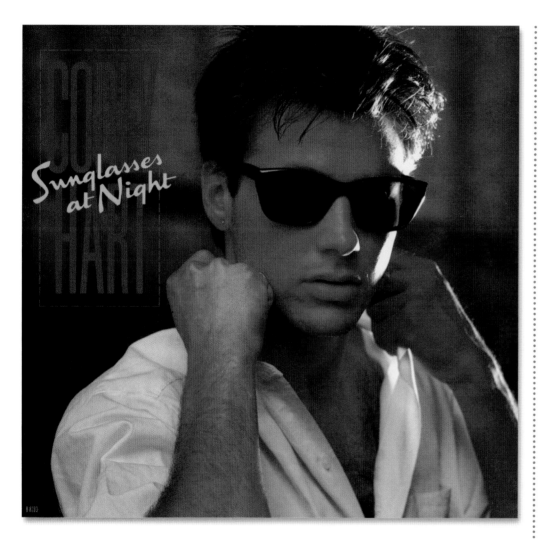

Whether you were a valley girl or boy toy, new waver or yuppie, one common accessory among the classes was a great pair of shades. Billy Idol and Corey Hart led the movement.

"Sunglasses at Night," in particular, became a cultural phenomenon and catch phrase. Hart recalls passing on several potential offers with advertisers (such as Ray-Ban). "In the '80s it was considered selling out to tie into product endorsement, so I foolishly turned them all down," says Hart. "How times have changed, eh?"

A true singer-songwriter at heart, Corey also passed on several songs that became soundtrack smashes in the '80s. "When I was a teenager I wanted to write my own songs and was influenced by artists like Billy Joel," explains Hart. "Therefore, recording someone else's original tune went against everything I believed in. I turned down some big hits in the process. I am also asked by artists like P. Diddy to sign off on interpolation versions [of 'Sunglasses at Night']...but I wrote the song whole and true at 19, and I just can't reconcile it being cut up in this way. I am sure someone hip like Gwen Stefani will do a great cover of it!"

"Sunglasses at Night" was a last minute add to his *First Offense* LP. Hart explains the motivation behind the hit: "The lyric on one hand was a story of deception in a relationship gone wrong by infidelity, but I was also trying to convey on a more existential level my teenage angst and rebellion at the world, and finding my place in it."

| The The | "Infected" | ARTWORK: **Andrew Johnson**
1986, Some Bizarre / TRUTH Q3 {12"}, U.K. |

the The the

infected

TRUTH Q3

Andy Johnson (a.k.a. "Andy Dog") was the longtime illustrator for The The, fronted by his brother Matthew. Andy's distinctive pieces, including his banned "Infected" artwork, frequently courted controversy.

"I consciously tried to make a drawing feel like a punch in the mouth," says Johnson.

Andy recalls the wrangling over "Infected": "I drew and painted that on my parents' dinner table, believe it or not. I kept it well-hidden from their eyes because they certainly wouldn't have been impressed."

"I had completed several drawings of angels and devils. They were variously crying, screaming, shooting up, and wanking (garden images of desperation and despair). Matt liked them and suggested mischievously that one image would be good for a single sleeve. So I drew it up. "

"In my work I've often asked questions about sex. Not the depiction of sex to titillate (i.e. porn) but questions about sex and love and how we relate to each other, what it means, and how it affects us."

"Matthew and Stevo [manager] both thought it was 'brilliant,' and so did, initially, the staff at CBS. Everyone was patting me on the back and making the predictable sort of jokes and comments."

"From what I remember the first thing I heard about it being 'banned' was that the ladies on the production line were refusing to handle it! I imagined a group of large, middle-aged dinner-lady types. And, to be honest, I had some sympathy...I could relate that to members of my own family."

"They asked me to re-crop it, and of course they paid me again, so I didn't mind. It's a terrible thing to admit, but the older you get the more you need money and principals and ideals go out the window."

The sleeve for "This Is the Day" was a bit more palatable for the masses. "I wandered around the Shoreditch and Spitalfields areas of East London photographing old buildings. I printed up the photos, copied them, cut them up, collaged them, and drew on them," says Johnson.

| Lita Ford | "Back to the Cave" | PHOTOGRAPHY: | Neil Preston |
| | | | 1988, Dreamland 8640, U.S. |

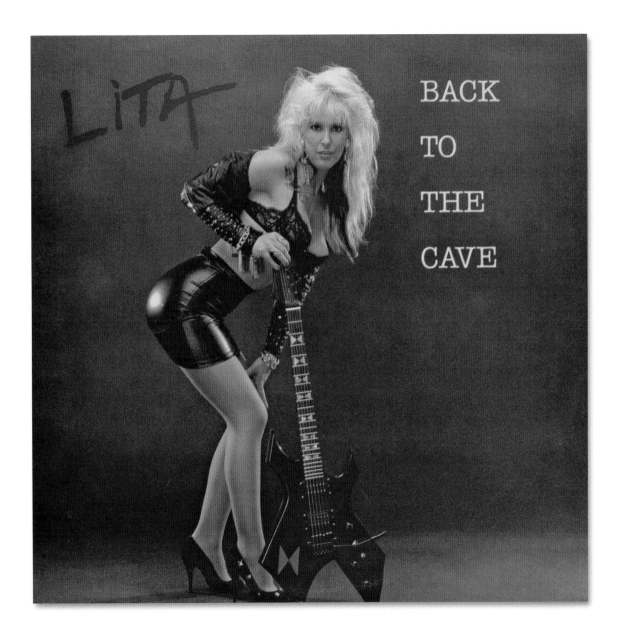

Vixen	"Cryin'"	PHOTOGRAPHY: Jeff Katz
		DESIGN: Artful Dodgers Ltd.
		1988, EMI / MTG 60, U.K.

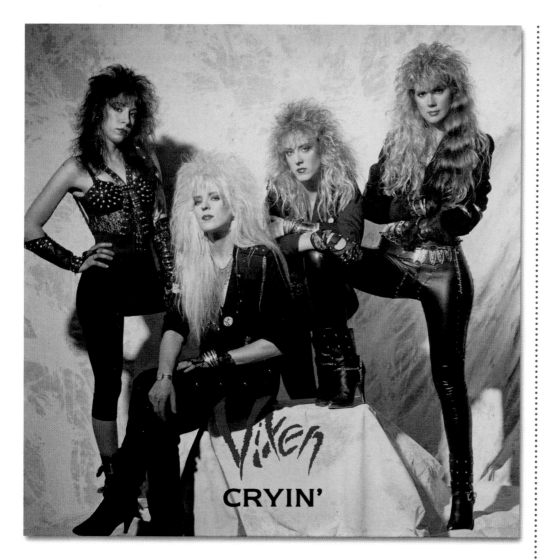

Vixen
CRYIN'

One of the last genres to remain a "boys club" in the '80s, hard rock had a steady stream of female breakthroughs by the end of the decade, including Lita Ford and Vixen.

"The crowds and audiences were always very supportive, and we never had a problem getting a gig," explains Jan Kuehnemund, Vixen guitarist and founding member. "But unfortunately the record execs had trouble being open minded about signing an all-female rock band. We heard it all. From 'is that really them playing all the instruments?' to 'girls should just sing and get guys to play the music.' We were surprised that the resistance was there, because we felt like a rock & roll band that just happened to be female."

Despite the industry skeptics, Vixen was able to maintain the upper hand regarding their image and more importantly, their music. "We were always in control," says Kuehnemund, "so we would wear things that we liked. However, I do remember from the 'Cryin'' shoot that my boots were killing me [laughing]. But it was definitely important for us that the music speak for itself. I'm not saying that image was unimportant, but because of the industry resistance to an all-female rock band we needed the music to speak the loudest."

Prince and The Revolution	"Pop Life"	PAINTING: **Doug Henders**
		ART DIRECTION: **Prince**
		DESIGN: **Laura LiPuma-Nash**
		1985, Paisley Park 28998, U.S.

Artist and designer Doug Henders worked extensively with Prince during the mid-'80s. This included the sleeve design for the Around the World in a Day *LP and the related* "Pop Life" *and* "Raspberry Beret" *singles.*

Henders details the experience: "I worked with Prince over a three-year period, from the Purple Rain *movie/tour up to* Under the Cherry Moon *movie pre-production, when I finally burned out."*

"Prince kept mostly to himself, being a creative genius, constantly writing, performing and recording. It was a great ride going on tour for a year and doing 101 shows in 30 cities, during which time I painted the album cover [*Around the World in a Day*; the single sleeves were cropped from that painting]. So, for me the artwork is very bound to the overall experience of being with a pop artist in his prime, being part of a phenomenon that touched many people personally, still to this day."

"I went to art school at Minneapolis College of Art and Design. About half-way through the production [of *Purple Rain*] they called me to make some paintings that were part of the script for the bedroom set. Prince fell in love with the work and asked if I would do a wall mural of one of my paintings in his recording studio; it also became the inner sleeve for the *Purple Rain* LP and was used as a backdrop for the *When Doves Cry* video."

"That summer ('84) Prince began rehearsing for the Purple Rain tour, and I was hired to work on the staging and go on the road to videotape the tour. After every show Prince would view the video in his suite, to tweak the performance and sound/lighting, but also to entertain late-night parties in his hotel suites with the local celebrities, from George Clinton and Bootsy Collins in Detroit to Madonna in New York. It was during this period that his personal manager Alan Leeds asked if I was interested in doing the cover art for Prince's new LP. The caveat was that they had already contracted a well-known artist but didn't give me his name (you [Matthew Chojnacki] are the first person who identified Jim Warren as being that artist)."

Prince and The Revolution	"Raspberry Beret"	PAINTING: Doug Henders ART DIRECTION: Prince DESIGN: Laura LiPuma-Nash 1985, Paisley Park 28972, U.S.

"Prince gave me a laundry list of characters and scenes disconnected from any narrative. It was sort of a Rorschach test to see how I would respond. I began making Polaroids of those around me from the tour, dressing them as characters. This included his Uncle Earl, the hairdresser (old man with the cane), Jerome Benton, Sheila E., and Susanna (Wendy's twin sister). I also had myself photographed (the guy in the cloud suit) determined to make a cameo. I put Prince's likeness on half a dozen of the characters (in a reverse Rorschach meant to appeal to his ego)."

"Prince never gave me specific influences, but I could guess some of them. I think the little child was inspired from the famous Vietnam photo. The apple is original sin and also the Beatles. One of the images was of Clara Bowe, the 20s film siren that he specifically requested. Another character was Chick, his ex-pro wrestler personal body guard. However, during the course of the tour he had a falling out and Prince had me remove him from the painting. He recognized that I used Sheila E. as a model and he smiled and then told me to draw a mustache on her. Also, if you look at the background [of the original LP cover] it is a silhouette of a female torso with legs and breast. Prince liked the subliminal touches."

"I would shoot concerts at night, party after the shows, and then go to my hotel suite to paint until the sun came up. I tried painting during the day but Prince would call me all hours at night to bring up the painting in progress to show it off to his girlfriends and pals. 'Here is my artist Doug.' Then he would say yes, yes, yes, no, yes. But mostly he was supportive."

"When we traveled I made management buy a ticket for the painting so it had its own seat. Otherwise it would have been damaged. It became my baby."

"We also traveled with our own basketball backboard and had pickup games wherever we went. Prince was about 5' 4" but he had a good jump shot. Of course, nobody would really try to block his shot."

Jane Wiedlin	"World on Fire"	PHOTOGRAPHY: Xavier Guardans
		DESIGN: Vivid I.D.
		1990, EMI 2039297, Italy

The Go-Go's were the first all-female band to achieve enduring success with a series of hits including "We Got the Beat," "Vacation," and "Head over Heels."

Going against the trends at the time, the band rarely used photographs on their cover artwork, instead opting for faceless graphic design.

The Go-Go's Kathy Valentine: "We were always conscious of the fact that photographs would date us. We didn't want artwork on recordings to signal any specific era. Looking back, it was a smart move because the '80s had some rather *distinctive* fashion and hair statements!"

Valentine and Go-Go's guitarist/keyboardist Charlotte Caffey co-wrote "Head over Heels," which featured Caffey in a striking piano solo. "Charlotte started the song," says Valentine, "and we both locked into the idea of what a whirlwind our lives had become in The Go-Go's."

Following the dissolution of the band in 1984, all members went on to other successful projects: Belinda Carlisle had a series of solo hits (e.g., "Mad About You," "Heaven Is a Place on Earth"); Jane Wiedlin released solo material and took up acting (*Clue*, *Bill & Ted's Excellent Adventure*); Caffey led her own band (The Graces) and collaborated with other artists including Jewel; Gina Shock worked with the likes of a-ha and John Mellencamp; and Kathy Valentine played in several bands, including World's Cutest Killers with Kelly Johnson of Girlschool fame.

The Go-Go's reunited in 1990, and have since balanced their solo careers with group performances and recordings.

Culture Club	"Church of the Poison Mind"	PHOTOGRAPHY: Mark Lebon / Julie Harrington
		DESIGN: Nick Egan
		1983, Virgin / VS 571, U.K.

Trendsetting, gender-bending Boy George of Culture Club stood out from his pop contemporaries with his controversial style and razor-sharp wit. Legions of fans (including some metal bands) followed George's lead and adopted a similar look.

"Church of the Poison Mind" and "It's a Miracle" were the first and fifth international hit singles released from Culture Club's *Colour by Numbers* LP (in between were "Karma Chameleon," "Victims," and "Miss Me Blind").

Prior to Culture Club, George was briefly a member of Bow Wow Wow (as "Lieutenant Lush"), while drummer Jon Moss previously worked with Adam And The Ants.

Rockwell	"Somebody's Watching Me"	ART DIRECTION:	Johnny Lee
		DESIGN:	Janet Levinson
			1983, Motown 61313, France

Peering artwork was used for Rockwell's "Somebody's Watching Me" and Animotion's "Obsession."

An alternate cover was originally intended for the Rockwell release. Art director Johnny Lee discusses the controversy surrounding the initial sleeve: "Since 'Somebody's Watching Me' was such a novel song, we [originally] decided on a light-hearted, almost cartoon-quality to the cover. We built a set with a room that had giant probing eyes as windows, with lighting that was dark and very Franz Kafka/ George Tooker-like. Rockwell was reading from a book titled *Paranoid?* and was eating a bleak and bland frozen TV dinner with a repressed expression."

"With this concept in hand, the sleeve was approved by management, talent, project managers, etc. and ready to go out to our color separator."

"My last approval was to come from the president of the label. At the time he had only one theory about album covers: large, bold (preferably all caps) type at the very top, and the artist's photo as large as possible. He approved all the album covers in his dark office and was also slightly color blind—just what every record company art director wants!"

Animotion	"Obsession"	DESIGN: Unknown
		1985, Mercury 76230 {12"}, Canada

"He went absolutely ballistic on me and started ranting and raving about not wanting to put Rockwell on the cover since he was black, and that Motown now had a 'white/crossover' pop hit on their hands. He thought pop radio wouldn't consider taking a chance on a new and unproven urban artist, and didn't want to alienate the younger white audiences. I thought I was back in the suppressed '60s again."

"It was now an extremely tight deadline, so Janet [Levinson, design] and I had only the rest of that afternoon to redesign the sleeve, front and back. With no time to think/experiment with a new design, we decided to give him exactly what he wanted... big, bold and red, all caps 'Rockwell' and only a hint of Rockwell's eyes in black-and-white against a black background. This way it was racially ambiguous and would appeal to both pop and urban audiences."

"After the single broke large and Motown felt secure with the success of Rockwell, they eventually ended up marketing him with color photos and all, as...'Rockwell.'"

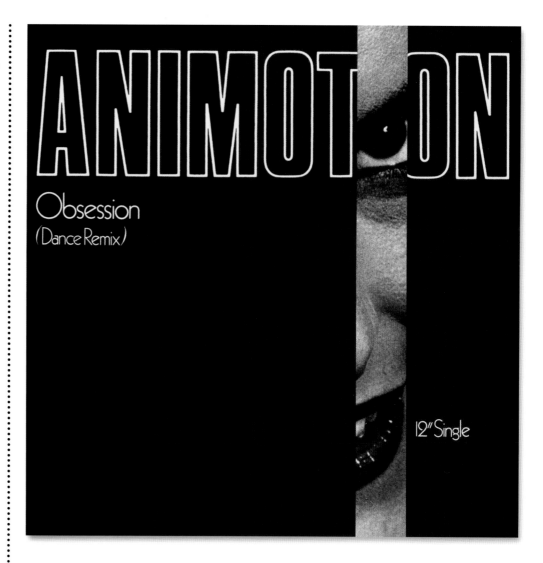

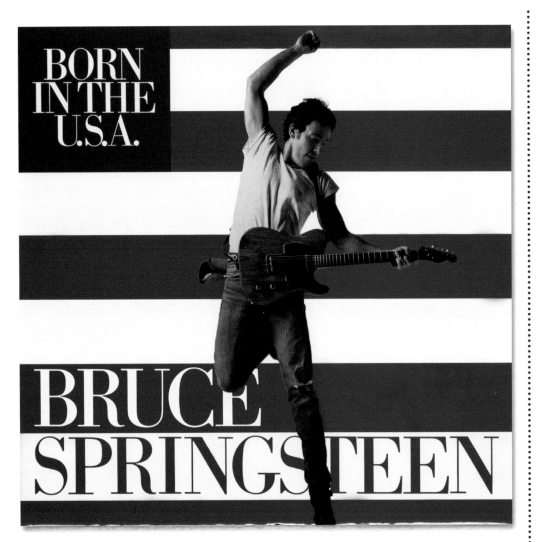

Bruce Springsteen's "Born in the U.S.A." and Lisa Stansfield's "What Did I Do to You?" both effectively enlisted bold striping to grab attention.

Springsteen's sleeve was seemingly all-American, but the song related to the after-effects of Vietnam rather than being a patriotic anthem. Ronald Reagan even misinterpreted the lyrics and adopted it as his 1984 political campaign theme until Springsteen requested that he stop using the song.

Lisa Stansfield	"What Did I Do to You?"	PHOTOGRAPHY: **Rocky Schenck** DESIGN: **Michael - Nash Associates** 1990, Arista 663168 {CD}, U.K.

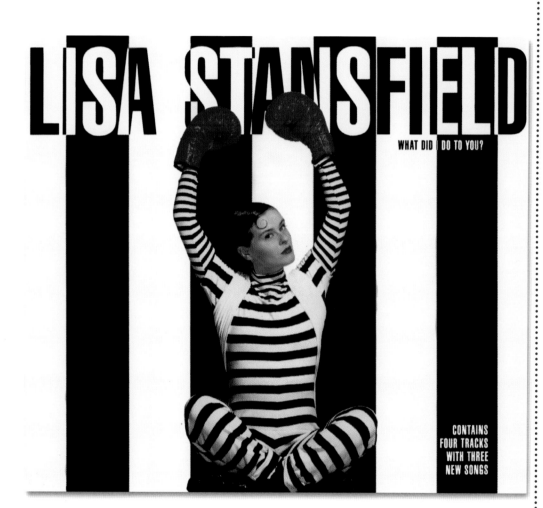

Stansfield's black-and-white stunner was the idea of costume designer Catherine Chambaret. "I originally used the gloves for a shoot with Jean-Baptiste Mondino and they became one of my favorite props. Also, I had a lot of black-and-white striped fabric since my assistant and I were often making clothing for music videos when the budgets were tight. We mixed a sweater with a jumpsuit on top, and added a white wrap around the bust for a more fitted look - that was the inspiration of the moment! We shot in my house, originally in the garden, but then moved to the living room. Lisa was so easy and enthusiastic."

Photographer Rocky Schenck: "Strangely enough, I had never seen this single cover until you [Matthew Chojnacki] contacted me. The record company never sent me a copy. It was great to finally see it. The photo shoot instigated a long relationship with the wonderful Lisa Stansfield. I ended up directing several of her videos, including *Never, Never Gonna Give You Up* and *The Line*."

Dueling comic-style sleeves from synthpop's Heaven 17 and thrash metal's Anthrax.

Heaven 17 was formed after Martyn Ware's and Ian Craig Marsh's exit from the original lineup of The Human League. The pop trio scored hits with "Let Me Go" and "Temptation," among others.

"Height of the Fighting" artist Jill Mumford: "I was an illustrator working freelance for *NME* at the time. I loved pop artist Lichtenstein's work, but was also inspired by some bikers I had just met (hence the leather look to the costume and the 'Death Or Glory' logo). I went to a demonstration with them against having to wear crash helmets. I was pillion and a policeman said to me, right outside Holloway women's prison, 'See you in there later!' (meaning that I would be arrested sooner or later). Very exciting times."

Anthrax

"I Am the Law"

ILLUSTRATION: Charlie Benante
COLORING: Scott Ian
1986, Island / 12 IS 316 {12"}, U.K.

Anthrax, one of the first bands to combine heavy metal with rap, is considered one of the "big four" thrash metal bands, along with Metallica, Megadeth, and Slayer.

Anthrax front man Scott Ian on "I Am the Law": "I was a big fan of Judge Dredd, and was reading *Dredd* when he was still in the [British science fiction comic] *2000 A.D.* The lyrics are obviously all about Dredd, and we were able to acquire the rights to use his image for the artwork. Charlie [Benante, drummer] did the art for the cover and the individual band member portraits that were part of the twelve-inch limited edition poster sleeve in the U.K. I did the coloring."

Ian continues on the state of cover artwork, "These days you don't see really great art any more. Downloading a booklet is not the same as being able to hold a twelve-inch cover in your hand."

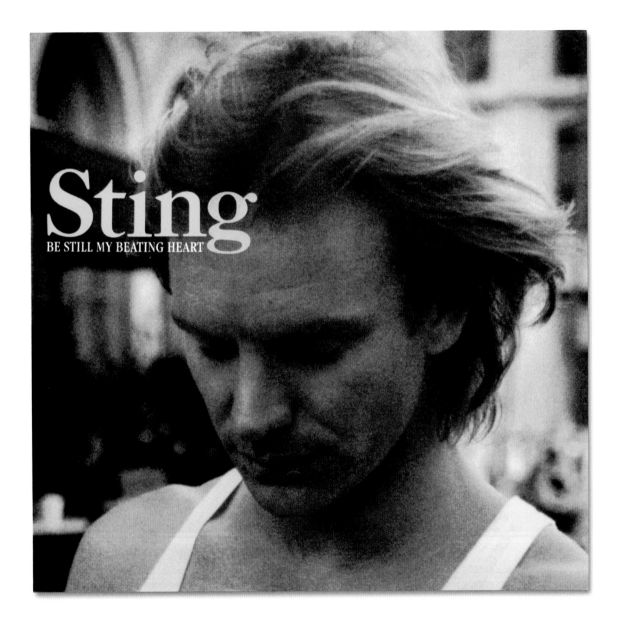

Gritty photographs with beige and green hues conveyed expressions of love on Sting's "Be Still My Beating Heart" and Steve Winwood's "Higher Love."

"Higher Love" won the Grammy for Record of the Year in 1986, besting a romance-filled category that included "Addicted to Love" (Robert Palmer) and "Greatest Love of All" (Whitney Houston).

Following the split of The Police in 1984, Sting went solo with a string of hits including "If You Love Somebody Set Them Free" and "We'll Be Together."

| **Pink Floyd** | "When the Tigers Broke Free" | ILLUSTRATION: | **Gerald Scarfe**
1982, Columbia 03142, U.S. |

British illustrator Gerald Scarfe (formerly a cartoonist for *The New Yorker* and *The Sunday Times*) worked with Pink Floyd on several aspects of *The Wall*. This included the album and single covers, as well as the film's animation.

"I was pleasantly surprised when I met the band in the early '70s," says Scarfe. "They were not what I expected —they were quite laid back and civilized, not rowdy and typical rockers."

The Wall's artwork is arguably the most celebrated in rock history, but initially Scarfe was modest about its potential. "I didn't realize that I was working on something special," says Scarfe, "To me it was just another job, albeit with exciting prospects. So, the awareness came after the public reception."

Following his extensive work with Pink Floyd, Scarfe left the rock music scene. "I was approached by several other bands for artwork, but none of them of the stature of Pink Floyd. So I pushed my work more into opera, theatre, ballet, and film."

Bryan Adams	"Hidin' from Love"	PHOTOGRAPHY: Mark Hanauer
		DESIGN: Chuck Beeson
		1980, A&M 7659, The Netherlands

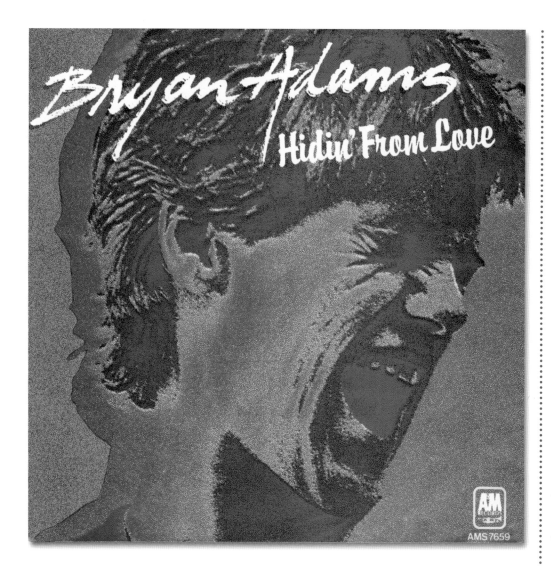

Scarfe's famous "scream" illustration (inspired by the anxiety of the character Pink in the film) seemed to influence other music-related pieces at the time. This included the sleeve for Bryan Adams' pre-fame dance single "Hidin' from Love."

Rammellzee vs. K-Rob

"Beat Bop"

ILLUSTRATION: Jean-Michel Basquiat
1983, Tartown 001 {12"}, U.S.

Famed African-American painter Jean-Michel Basquiat first gained notoriety as a New York City graffiti artist, and later became an international sensation as a neo-expressionist until his sudden death in 1988. The Warhol protégé's pieces, which fetch in the tens of millions of dollars, continue to heavily influence modern art.

Basquiat also occasionally dabbled in music. This included his production work on the classic old-school rap track "Beat Bop" (the theme to *Style Wars*). Original pressings of the sleeve, which included artwork by Basquiat, make it the most valuable hip-hop sleeve of all time.

"['Beat Bop'] was, and still is a hip-hop classic...and Basquiat needed some good words," says "Beat Bop" rapper Rammellzee. "It was a test piece, so I didn't think much of it. Only 10,000 copies were made at first, and Basquiat would hand them out at clubs here in New York...and the cover's just ugly," quips Rammellzee.

Sonic Youth

"Stick Me Donna
Magick Momma"

ILLUSTRATION: Savage Pencil
1988, Fierce / FRIGHT 015/016, U.K.

Similarly featuring a black-and-white sketch, indie designer Savage Pencil designed "Stick Me Donna Magick Momma," a Sonic Youth bootleg.

"Steve from Fierce Recordings mentioned one day that he was planning a Sonic Youth single and asked if I would be interested in doing the cover," explains Savage Pencil's Edwin Pouncey. "Fierce Recordings was a label that did tiny runs, most of which were taken from various sources. Other Fierce releases included material by Charles Manson, Seeds founder Sky Saxon, and early Velvet Underground drummer, shaman, and poet Angus MacLise. Steve's attitude appealed to me so I happily agreed to do the art for him."

"My inspiration for the cover was a mixture of surrealism and goony cartoon art. A kind of Salvador Dali meets Hanna-Barbera mix where the members of the group were depicted as half-formed characters in an episode of Scooby-Doo on acid...or something. There were two versions, one with the drawing printed in black, and the other in a congealed blood color."

Flat graphic art (with one exposed nipple each) was used for the Motel's "Danger" (released prior to their smash "Only the Lonely") and Baltimora's "Tarzan Boy."

"'Danger' was never supposed to be a Motels single," says lead Martha Davis, "I actually wrote it for The Pointer Sisters."

Davis continues, "I found the artwork in a thrift store book called The Decorative Arts of the Forties and Fifties: Austerity/Binge, by Bevis Hillier. The artwork was originally a 1973 oil painting by Duggie Fields. One of the few color plates in the book, it immediately grabbed my attention."

"Capitol was always very supportive of my choice of artwork, and didn't grumble too much. At one point I had a dress and hat made to emulate the painting. However, the appliqué, which was made to simulate the breast, looked more like a fried egg. Not really what I had in mind!"

| U2 | "I Will Follow (Live)" | DESIGN: Unknown |
| | | 1982, Island 10452, The Netherlands |

"I Will Follow" was the first track on U2's debut LP *Boy*. While the pre-fame single didn't race up the charts, it was an immediate fan favorite in concert, becoming the band's most-played live song alongside "Pride (In The Name Of Love)."

A live version of "I Will Follow" (shown here) was released in the Netherlands in '82. The cover photo was from U2's Werchter, Belgium, show on July 4, 1982, and shows Bono hoisting a white flag that he received from a fan.

| Texas | "Prayer for You" | PHOTOGRAPHY: **Pennie Smith**
DESIGN: **Jules Balme**
1989, Mercury / TEX 4, U.K. |

TEXAS

PRAYER FOR YOU

A similar black-and-white crowd shot was used for Texas' "Prayer for You." Jules Balme designed the cover.

"Texas was a case of 'we want the guys who designed the Clash' (Transvision Vamp was a similar situation) and not an unreasonable idea, given the legacy of the band by then," says Balme. "They were keen to be seen as a group, and not trade off Sharleen as the typical good looking front woman. As a result, Pennie [Smith, photography] did a number of shoots with the band—rehearsal studios, video shoots, and gigs. We took the angle that each sleeve would be an issue of *Life* magazine and would feature a different group member in a reportage style."

Balme continues, "This was the fourth single and guitarist Ally's second appearance on a cover. By the time the album was released, Sharleen had only appeared on a sleeve once. That all changed once I lost the gig."

Comic-style artwork was used for pioneering hip-hop and funk artists Afrika Bambaataa and Bootsy Collins.

Afrika Bambaataa, best known for the classic track "Planet Rock," created the "electro-funk" sound by combining Kraftwerk-inspired techno with hip-hop. "Renegades of Funk" was covered by Rage Against the Machine in 2000.

| Bootsy's Rubber Band | "Body Slam!" | ILLUSTRATION: Steve Miller
DESIGN: Bootsy Collins
LOGO: Michael Manoogian
1982, Warner Bros. 29919 {12"}, U.S. |

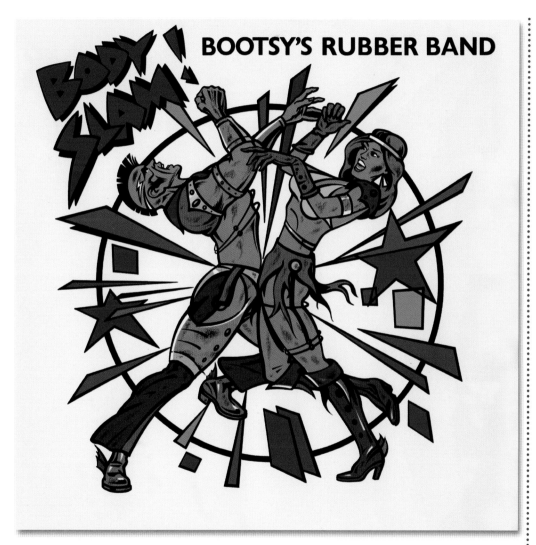

Funk bassist and fashion maven Bootsy Collins was a member of George Clinton's Parliament/ Funkadelic when he formed Bootsy's Rubber Band. He later collaborated as a solo artist with Deee-Lite ("Groove Is in the Heart") and Snoop Dogg, among others.

Rick Astley

"Together Forever"

PHOTOGRAPHY: Paul Cox
DESIGN: Mainartery
1988, RCA 8319, U.S.

Johnny Hates Jazz | "Shattered Dreams"

PHOTOGRAPHY: Simon Fowler
DESIGN: Stylorouge
1988, Virgin 99383, U.S.

johnny hates **JAZZ**

Fellow Brits Rick Astley and Johnny Hates Jazz left the makeup and spandex in the '80s closet to maintain dapper, clean-cut images.

Johnny Hates Jazz frontman Clark Datchler discusses the pluses and minuses of being cast as the visual focal point for the band: "Our first single ['Me and My Foolish Heart'] had not been a commercial success. The main image [on that sleeve] was of a professor-like character screaming, as a visual depiction of 'Johnny Hates Jazz.' It was very tongue-in-cheek and in a way it worked, as JHJ came to be regarded as a highly credible band by the 'serious' music press in Britain at that time."

"This continued with the release of 'Shattered Dreams.' No one knew what we looked like...that is, until the single entered the U.K. Top 20. As soon as we appeared on TV, an impression seemed to be formed by both record label and media. Suddenly, we were visually marketable, for better and for worse. On the upside, 'Shattered Dreams' went on to become a huge hit worldwide, and the three of us were ecstatic. On the downside, we began to be criticized by our former-supporters in the media, which seemed to be a reflection of our image, not our music. This was disappointing. However, I think our 'look' did us more good than harm, and feel the image helped us maintain a sense of style and dignity in a business where it is all too easy to sacrifice such attributes on the warpath to success."

Datchler did not anticipate "Shattered Dreams'" success. "When you're in the midst of writing a song, it's often hard to keep a perspective as to what is strong about it and what is not. The very first person who told me that 'Shattered Dreams' was going to be a hit was my Dad, who had been a successful jazz musician many years before. I think that his approval gave me a deep sense of confidence with the song."

Debbie Harry and Lenny Kravitz both have their fingers firmly placed on the pulse of the art and fashion worlds.

The cover for Debbie Harry's solo single "French Kissin' in the USA" was a collaboration between pop icon Andy Warhol and fashion designer Stephen Sprouse. Fascinated with life in Hollywood and the music industry, Warhol frequently painted celebrity portraits. Harry was one of his regular subjects.

| Lenny Kravitz | "Let Love Rule" | DESIGN: Inge Schaap |
| | | 1989, Virgin America / VUSTG 26 {12"}, U.K. |

Warhol's artwork from the '60s to the '80s had an immediate and indelible impact on other artists. The sleeve for Lenny Kravitz's debut single "Let Love Rule," for example, contained similar design elements to "French Kissin'."

"Andy Warhol was an amazing artist. Some of his work still feels very fresh to me," says Kravitz's designer Inge Schaap.

Schaap continues, "It was difficult not to go a little retro when you designed something for Lenny. He was very authentic and a great friend toward all of us in the art department. Everybody loved him. This was Lenny's very first single, so we wanted it to grab attention."

Divine	"Walk Like a Man"	PHOTOGRAPHY: Bill Bernardo
		DESIGN: The Bouncing Ball
		1985, Bellaphon 07329, Germany

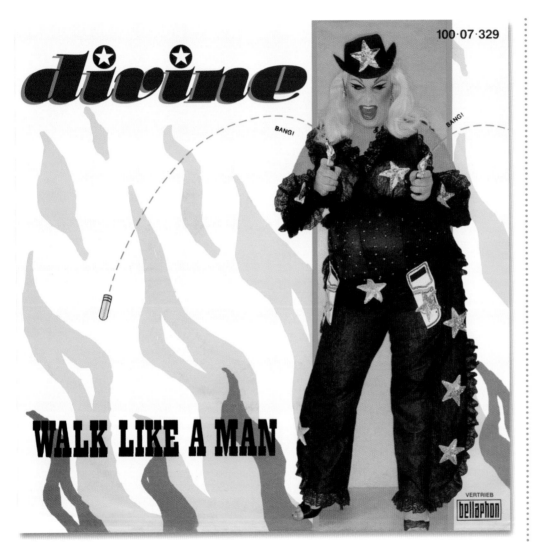

The king and queen of '80s shock: Divine and the Plasmatics' Wendy O. Williams.

While starring in numerous John Waters raunch classics such as *Pink Flamingos* and *Female Trouble*, drag queen Divine delivered musical camp with several dance hits including "Walk Like a Man."

The Plasmatics were formed by anti-artist (and Yale alum) Rod Swenson and fronted by the legendary Wendy O. Williams.

Swenson: "Art (by my way of thinking) falls into two generally opposing categories, the one which works directly or indirectly to empower the status quo (even if by simply going along with it), and the other which lives to assault it. Wendy O. Williams and the Plasmatics was the latter."

"At the core of what Wendy and I shared was revulsion for contemporary culture… its banality, conformity, consumerism, and consequences. Wendy lived to challenge the power structure, regardless of the repercussions; she was a true revolutionary. Her authenticity, among other things, made her a historically rare and utterly awesome person."

| Plasmatics | "Monkey Suit" | PHOTOGRAPHY: | **Butch Star**
1980, Stiff / Buy 91, U.K. |

"'Monkey Suit' was released early in our career, after we had our debut appearance in the U.K. where we planned to blow up a car and was banned. I shot the cover under the pseudonym 'Butch Star.' Wendy was featured as a dominatrix, before getting her famous mohawk, effectively bringing an establishment guy to his knees."

"The guy in the monkey suit was actually a member of our road crew named John Rockwell. When the *NY Times* critic by the same name refused to show up at some of our very early shows, we used a quote from our own John Rockwell in ads: 'the greatest rock band I have ever seen,' with small type saying, 'not with' and larger type saying, 'The *New York Times*' and then a small asterisk and very small type explaining who our John Rockwell was. People expressed amazement that such an apparently straight-laced critic in an establishment paper would have such a reaction."

"Such is the work of the Dadaist."

| Aneka | "Japanese Boy" | DESIGN: Unknown |
| | | 1981, Hansa 103349, Germany |

STEREO 103 349 - 100

HANSA

日本の男子

JAPANESE BOY

ANEKA

Being "big in Japan" was all the rage in the '80s, as seen with The Vapors' "Turning Japanese" and Aneka's "Japanese Boy." Both singles featured artwork with Japanese-style lettering and flat graphic art.

Following their smash singles, The Vapors and Aneka had a few more minor U.K. hits (Aneka's "Little Lady," The Vapors' "Jimmie Jones"). However, both acts folded by the early '80s.

The Vapors' members went on to careers in music law and television, while Mary Sandeman (Aneka) returned to her original calling, Scottish folk music, where she was already an accomplished artist.

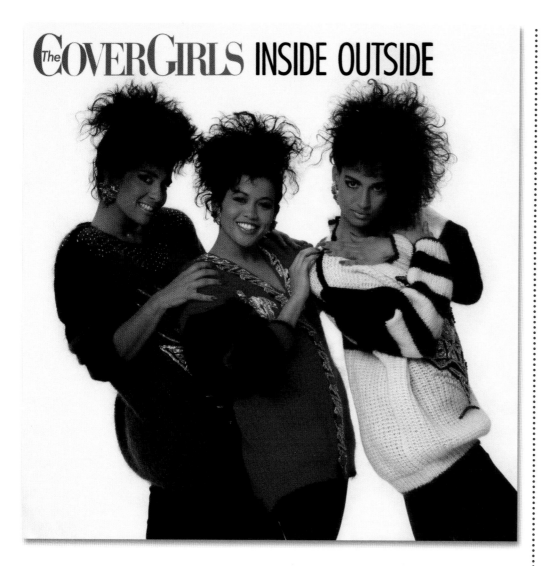

The CoverGirls INSIDE OUTSIDE

Two freestyle dance trios model classic '80s fashion trends.

Sweet Sensation ("Hooked on You," "Sincerely Yours") was outfitted here in 100% neon spandex, while The Cover Girls ("We Can't Go Wrong," "Show Me") wore over-sized sweater dresses…who didn't?

"It was all about the hair and the clothes," quips Sweet Sensation founding member Betty LeBron. "Bustiers and ruffled mini-skirts were the epitome of fashion, the more elaborate the better. Hair was…well…big and bold. Bold in height as well as color (frosted, platinum, or jet black with blue streaks). We kept the hairspray and color industry alive! The cover for 'Take It while It's Hot' was shot and styled after the supermodel trends. There was a new stretchy bandeau segmented tube dress style that was very hot then and made popular by Linda Evangelista and Naomi Campbell; the designer was Giorgio Sant'Angelo. Color was also hot. Bright, bold colors always made a statement. So, we paired up with big hair and hot colors and a 45 cover was born!"

| Bananarama | "Shy Boy" | DESIGN: Nick Egan / Peter Barrett
1983, London 810112, U.S. |

"Shy Boy" and "Dracula's Tango (Sucker for Your Love)" placed Bananarama and Toto Coelo in tongue-in-cheek graphic design settings.

Bananarama rocketed to fame when Fun Boy Three's Terry Hall saw the female trio in U.K.'s *The Face* magazine and admired their fashion sense. Hall subsequently asked them to guest on "T'aint What You Do (It's the Way that You Do It)," while Fun Boy Three returned the favor by backing Bananarama's "Really Saying Something."

Bananarama was an instant sensation, becoming the U.K.'s best-selling girl group of all time until the Spice Girls outsold them a decade later. Other international smashes included "Shy Boy" (shown there), "Cruel Summer," and "Venus."

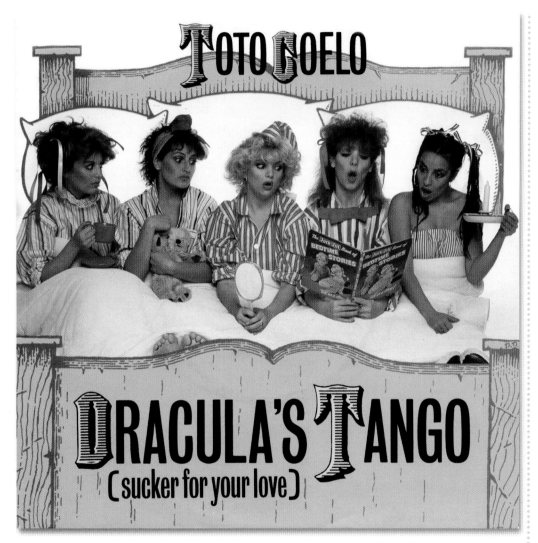

Toto Coelo (or Total Coelo in the U.S., to avoid confusion with the band Toto) had a slightly shorter life span. Their initial single "I Eat Cannibals Part 1" was an international hit, partially buoyed by their wildly colorful costumes and energetic personalities.

However, when their follow-ups "Dracula's Tango (Sucker For Your Love)" and "Milk From A Coconut" sputtered on the charts, the group began to dissolve, eventually downsizing to a trio, and then altogether.

| Men without Hats | "The Safety Dance" | DESIGN: B. Wear @ A.S.
1982, Statik / TAK 1, U.K. |

| Greg Kihn Band | "Jeopardy" | DESIGN: Unknown |
| | | 1983, Beserkley 969847, France |

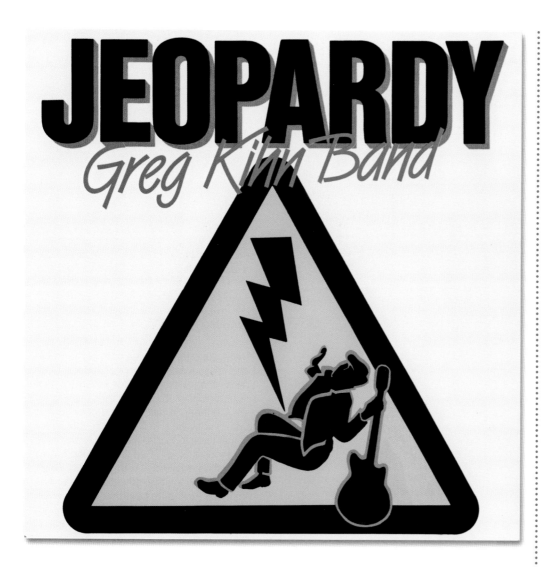

JEOPARDY
Greg Kihn Band

Two tales of '80s caution were found in the signature hits "The Safety Dance" and "Jeopardy."

While the cover for "The Safety Dance" showed a sock hop, the song actually referenced punk clubs that were banning pogo dancing at the time. Men without Hats lead Ivan Doroschuk: "[we were] getting kicked out of clubs every time a brave new DJ would play 'Heart Of Glass' or 'Planet Claire.'"

The name "Men without Hats" came to Doroschuk in a unforgettable dream sequence: "I had a dream where I formed a band called 'Men without Hate,' but when the posters for our first show came back from the printers they had misspelled the name of the band and printed 'Men without Hats' instead. The poster was René Magritte's *Ceci N'est Pas Une Pipe* ['this is not a pipe' in French], except that at the bottom it read 'This is not Men without Hats.' The dream was so convincing that when the time came I had no choice but to name my band that."

"The Safety Dance" has been referenced countless times in pop culture since '82, and Doroschuck enjoys the mentions. His favorite so far is "Beavis & Butt-head watching *The Safety Dance* video," says Doroschuck, "Butt-head: 'Is that Michael Jackson?...this butthole keeps saying he can dance, but it's like, he can't dance!'"

Greg Kihn also has a sense of humor with his band's music. Kihn appeared as himself, for example, in "Weird Al" Yankovic's parody video *I Lost on Jeopardy*.

Twisted Sister	"We're Not Gonna Take It"	PHOTOGRAPHY:	Mark Weiss
		ART DIRECTION:	Bob Defrin
		BONE LOGO:	Dee Snider / Suzette Guilot-Snider
			1984, Atlantic 89641, U.S.

b/w
YOU CAN'T STOP ROCK 'N' ROLL

Occasionally an album cover became so quickly iconic that it was also used for an associated single. Twisted Sister's "We're Not Gonna Take It" (from the Stay Hungry *album) and Quiet Riot's "Cum on Feel the Noize" (from* Metal Health*) are examples.*

"It was supposed to be a shot of the whole band," says Twisted Sister photographer Mark Weiss. "I shot the band for seven to eight hours, and then they left. Later that night I saw a bone in a deli, and the clerk gave it to me. I showed it to Dee and he stayed for another three to four hours. It was two or three in the morning, and Dee was making noises and getting aggressive with the prop. When the band saw the final cover, they were, like, 'What the fuck is he doing on the cover? It was supposed to be all of us.' They thought we had this planned the whole time, but of course we didn't."

| Quiet Riot | "Cum on Feel the Noize" | ILLUSTRATION: **Stan Watts**
ART DIRECTION: **Quiet Riot**
DESIGN: **Jay Vigon**
1983, Epic 3616, The Netherlands |

Quiet Riot founding member Frankie Banali on the "Cum on Feel the Noize" image: "We decided not to use a band picture for the cover since we were an unknown entity. We liked the idea of a 'mascot' in the sense of Iron Maiden's use of the 'Eddie' character, and the goal was to make the central figure a fan of the band (albeit one that is slightly off-center). We discussed the theme from the *Man in the Iron Mask* [and decided on a faceless image]. The obvious component was to put the character in a straightjacket. I had bought a red leather motorcycle jacket in 1980 while recording in Edinburgh, Scotland, and the model for the cover wore it backwards. Kevin [DuBrow] had the idea to have buttons with our faces on the jacket, making a 'fan' statement. It was a fairly low budget affair, and if you look closely, the 'padded cell' background is nothing more than a shipping blanket!"

FOREIGNER

WAITING FOR A GIRL LIKE YOU
FEELS LIKE THE FIRST TIME
COLD AS ICE

JOE JACKSON

steppin'out
B/W
chinatown

While Boy George and Pete Burns of Dead or Alive frequently turned heads with their feminine characteristics, women who dressed opposite of type in the '80s were deemed more palatable by the mainstream. A double standard?

Here a suit and tie worked just as well for both the female model on "Waiting for a Girl Like You" and for Joe Jackson.

Fronted by Lou Gramm ("Midnight Blue"), Foreigner led the arena rock movement with favorites including "I Want to Know What Love Is" and "I Don't Want to Live without You," while classical prodigy Joe Jackson carved his own musical niche by composing pop with a symphonic flare, as heard on "Steppin' Out."

| Toyah | "Ieya" | PHOTOGRAPHY: Gered Mankowitz
1982, Safari / SAFE(L)28 {12"}, U.K. |

| Visage | "Fade to Grey" | PHOTOGRAPHY: Robyn Beeche |
| | | 1980, Polydor / POSPX 194 {12"}, U.K. |

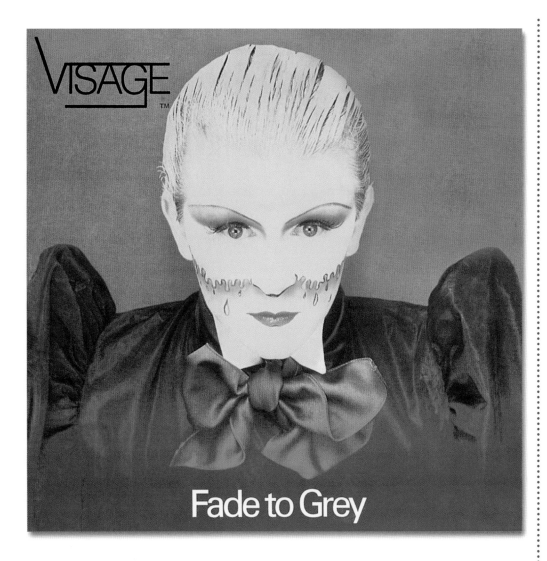

VISAGE ™

Fade to Grey

Very few artists have the ability to turns heads just by being, but Toyah Willcox and Visage's Steve Strange did just that. Their faces were continuously changing canvases that grabbed attention.

Visage photographer Robyn Beeche recalls the inspiration for "Fade to Grey": "Cross-dressing became fashionable in the early '80s, and the greatest androgyny of them all, cult icon Divine, came to perform on stage and in clubs throughout the U.K. I met [Visage frontman] Steve Strange at the Blitz Club in Covent Garden, and felt that this androgynous approach was perfect for his 'Fade to Grey' sleeve."

"I wanted to create a timeless and universally accepted photograph," says Beeche, "and to create an illusion that caught people's attention. Push processing of the film helped achieve its painterly quality, and Australian makeup artist Richard Sharah designed the 'dripping face,' which worked well the title."

Steve Strange collaborated on the shoot. "Steve had an insatiable appetite for being photographed," explains Beeche, "he understood the publicity machine and how to utilize imagery well.

Playground Twist · Siouxsie and the Banshees

Leading the way in the late-70s and early-80s indie music scene were post-punk outfits Siouxsie and the Banshees and Echo and the Bunnymen.

Early singles "Playground Twist" and "The Pictures on My Wall" were housed in gritty, hand-drawn sleeves.

"Playground Twist" was the third single from Siouxsie and the Banshees. It was the only single released from their second LP, *Join Hands*, and followed their breakthrough hits "Hong Kong Garden" and "The Staircase (Mystery)."

| Echo and the Bunnymen | "The Pictures on My Wall" | DESIGN: Unknown |
| | | 1979, Zoo / CAGE 004, U.K. |

"The Pictures on My Wall" was initially released in a limited run of only 4,000 copies. The single was recorded prior to drummer Pete de Freitas joining the band, and was subsequently re-recorded (with Pete on drums) for their debut LP *Crocodiles*.

| Janet Jackson | "Nasty" | ART DIRECTION: Chuck Beeson
DESIGN: Melanie Nissen
1986, A&M 2830, U.K. |

Hazel O'Connor's "Time" and Janet Jackson's "Nasty" both contained similar black-and-white elements offset by boldly colored geometric forms.

"Time" was designed by Edward Bell, best known for David Bowie's *Scary Monsters (and Super Creeps)* LP sleeve.

"Nasty" was designed by Melanie Nissen: "Recording artists always had final approval of their artwork (it was an unwritten law), as they should, sometimes for better or for worse. I remember Janet coming to look at everything, but her father, Janet's manager at the time, had not [reviewed the cover] until the very end of the process when it was going to press. He asked, 'How could you make my daughter's name so small and plain on the cover? It doesn't look big and important.' I tried to explain that big type doesn't always mean important, and that the whole package looked strong in a different way."

"But, alas, time was on my side and it was too late to change. The singles, ads, posters, etc. were all generated from the front LP cover."

"I admired Janet's decision to do something fresh and modern at the time—the music was great. I don't think people realized what a smash the album would be."

Whitney Houston

"I Wanna Dance with Somebody (Who Loves Me)"

PHOTOGRAPHY: **Richard Avedon**
DESIGN: **Marl Larson**
1987, Arista 9598, U.S.

Writers George Merrill and Shannon Rubicam penned Whitney Houston's early pop hits "How Will I Know" and "I Wanna Dance with Somebody (Who Loves Me)."

Rubicam: "Shortly after signing with Almo Irving Publishing in 1983, we were asked to write a song for Janet Jackson, and we came up with 'How Will I Know.' Alas, she was working with Jimmy Jam and Terry Lewis on *Control*, and she passed. [At the same time] Clive Davis was looking for material for a young singer named Whitney Houston. He loved it."

"[Following 'How Will I Know's' success] Clive called us with a request to write another song for Whitney's second album, and of course we were thrilled to comply," says Rubicam. "He listened to our demo of 'I Wanna Dance…' and wanted the song, but thought it might be better with sexier lyrics. Although we disagreed, we did give him a different lyrical version, but Whitney ended up recording the original lyrics in the end. We haven't been able to find the revised lyric…just as well. Whitney sang her body and soul into it, and that's what counts in the end."

PHOTOGRAPHY: **Lester Cohen**
1986, Atlantic 86797 {12"}, U.S.

Merrill and Rubicam had yet another song, "Waiting for a Star to Fall," in the works for Houston's third LP. However, at the time Houston was moving on from her lighthearted pop image, which paralleled Stacey Q and other pop stars of the moment, and ultimately passed on the track. "Whitney was intending to make a more R&B-based album [*I'm Your Baby Tonight*]," says Rubicam, "and 'Waiting for a Star to Fall' would have indeed been too pop to fit in with that notion."

Merrill and Rubicam subsequently decided to release the single themselves under the guise Boy Meets Girl. It was a Top 5 smash. "We hoped and dreamed [for a hit], but I would say expectation was not in the mental mix," remarks Rubicam. "We were appropriately blown away by the level of success the song reached, and its endurance through a couple of decades of covers and remixes."

Director John Hughes had quite the knack for choosing that perfect song for his classic '80s films, including Simple Minds' "Don't You (Forget about Me)" in The Breakfast Club, Thompson Twins' "If You Were Here" in Sixteen Candles, and Yello's "Oh Yeah" in Ferris Bueller's Day Off.

One of the biggest hits from a Hughes film was "If You Leave." OMD's Andy McCluskey recounts the story: "I got the impression that John Hughes was a big fan of British bands, and asked a lot of us to contribute to his movies. He specifically asked for OMD to write a song for *Pretty in Pink*, which completely flattered us."

"We were invited to the *Pretty in Pink* set, met Jon Cryer, Molly Ringwald, and John Hughes, and watched them film one of the scenes. They subsequently gave us a script, saying that they needed a big epic song for the film's prom finale. Their only proviso was that it needed to be the same tempo as Simple Minds' 'Don't You (Forget about Me),' since the final scene had already been cut to that song."

"So, we went away and wrote a song… called 'Goddess of Love,' written based on the original script that had Molly Ringwald ending up with Jon Cryer's character Duckie. We turned up with our two-inch tape ready to mix, and they responded, 'yeah, we like the song, but lyrically it doesn't make sense anymore because we changed the ending. All the girls in the audience during our tests said that they liked Duckie, but wanted Andie to end up with the good-looking kid."

"So, there we were In L.A., two days to spare before we went on tour with the Thompson Twins, and they asked us to write another song. Off the tops of our heads we wrote 'If You Leave,' laying it down in one day, finished at three or four in the morning, and sending it by courier overnight to John Hughes at Paramount. We got a phone call at 9 AM from our manager saying 'John loves the demo— finish it!' So we ran back in the studio."

"When I went to the premiere, we were like, 'Shit, it [the prom scene, and song] goes on, and on, and on.' We had no idea that it was going to be used so extensively. It helped 'If You Leave' become, by a mile, our biggest hit in the states."

"We were so thrilled to be involved with the film. Hughes' films captured a snapshot of an era in terms of teen culture, fashion, and music, but there's a timeless element to it. Teen relationships never change, even though the soundtrack, clothing, and haircuts do."

Also pictured: Flesh for Lulu's "I Go Crazy" from the Hughes flick *Some Kind of Wonderful.*

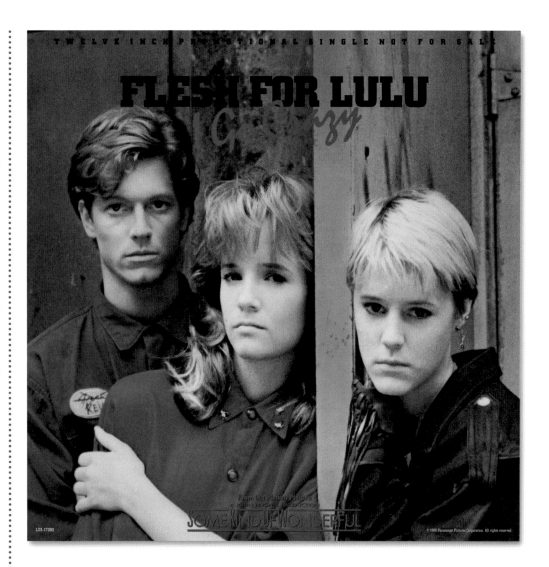

| Misfits | "Die, Die My Darling" | MISFITS LOGO: Pushead
1984, Plan 9 / PL9-03 {12"}, U.S. |

The Misfits defined the horror punk genre, which merged horror themes and images with punk rock music.

The band's "Die, Die My Darling" sleeve, for example, was adapted from a cover of the comic book *Chamber of Chills* (#19, September, 1953), a '50s series that outraged with its frequent depictions of torture, decapitations, atomic bombs, and other evils. It is also worth noting that the Misfits' iconic logo here was hand-drawn by artist Pushead, who illustrated for Metallica, Ministry, and Queensrÿche.

| Whodini | "The Haunted House of Rock" | DESIGN: Unknown |
| | | 1983, Jive 34, U.K. |

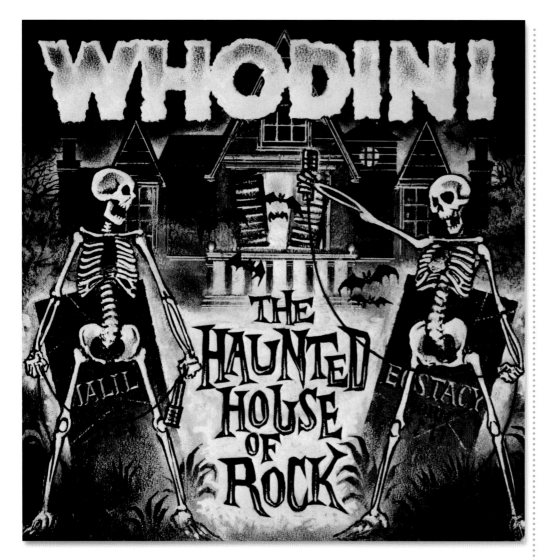

Whodini likewise tapped into the horror theme (a bit more whimsically) with their debut single "The Haunted House of Rock." Managed by Russell Simmons, Whodini broke early hip-hop ground at mainstream radio with songs including "Freaks Come Out at Night" and the Thomas Dolby-produced "Magic's Wand." They also ushered in the new jack swing sound of the late '80s by being one of the first groups to mix rap with R&B.

Jesus Jones	"Info Psycho"	PHOTOGRAPHY: Simon Fowler DESIGN: Stylorouge 1989, Food / 12FOODX18 {12"}, U.K.

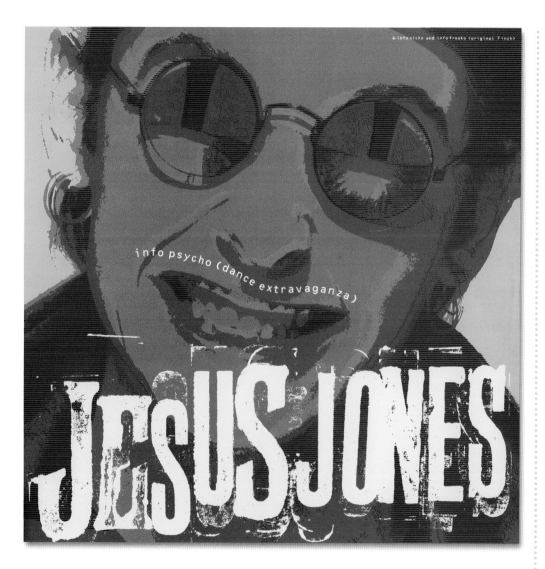

Psychedelic Furs and Jesus Jones pushed the boundaries of pop radio. The Furs brought forward a punk influence, while Jesus Jones mixed dance and hip-hop with indie rock.

Both groups also released an impressive series of sleeve images. Psychedelic Furs' covers were often at the helm of Richard Butler, who later ventured into fine art, while Jesus Jones' pieces were designed by image powerhouse Stylorouge.

Rob O'Connor of Stylorouge: "I thought what Jesus Jones was doing was very exciting at the time. They were riding the crest of a rock-dance music wave, along with EMF and Pop Will Eat Itself. Food Records were putting a lot of effort into Jesus Jones, and wanted interesting images of lead singer Mike Edwards for the 'Info Freako' and 'Info Psycho' single covers. We always put our ideas together first, and in amongst the concepts was a 1962 photograph by Richard Avedon [*Killer Joe Piro, Dance Teacher*], which they all responded really well to. This was pre-computer, so we did a lot of messing around in the darkroom for a similar effect. The sleeve was quite colorful. They deliberately wanted to create a ravey, dance, rock, trippy sleeve, and of course 'psycho' came from psychedelic."

While Jesus Jones later scored more mainstream hits with "Right Here, Right Now" and "Real Real Real," it was "Info Freako" ("Info Psycho" was a remix) that initially created a buzz with critics and moved the indie dance genre forward.

| Fat Boys | "Are You Ready for Freddy" | PHOTOGRAPHY: Nancy Brown
DESIGN: Lynda West
FREDDIE KRUEGER: New Line Cinema
1988, Tin Pan Apple 887894, U.S. |

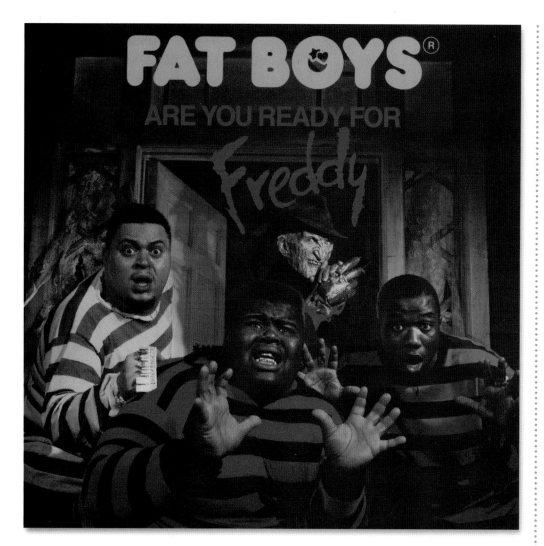

Horror icon Freddy Krueger was inescapable in 1988. He was on the big screen, in your dreams, and even at radio, as comedic rappers Fat Boys and DJ Jazzy Jeff & The Fresh Prince both took turns at creating A Nightmare on Elm Street-*inspired anthems.*

Originally called the Disco 3, Brooklyn schoolmates Mark "Prince Markie Dee" Morales, Darren "The Human Beat Box" Robinson, and Damon "Kool Rock-Ski" Wimbley landed a record deal after winning a talent competition at Radio City Music Hall; their story was largely the basis for the film *Krush Groove*. Hits included "All You Can Eat" and "Jail House Rap," both produced by Kurtis Blow.

Kool Rock-Ski: "The '80s were a good time for rap music, and even better for Buff, Markie, and me. Basically, we chose things that felt right. 'Wipeout,' 'The Twist,' 'Louie Louie,' 'Are You Ready for Freddy,' those were no brainers."

Prince Markie Dee: "Back in the day, who didn't love them some *Nightmare on Elm Street*? When the movie producers stepped up and asked 'you interested in a Freddy Krueger track?', we were like, 'does Buff like eating three pizzas [laughs]?' Freddy Krueger, scary faced dude, that's my boy right there! Then came the video shoot. My son Little Mark was so scared of Freddy."

D.J. Jazzy Jeff & The Fresh Prince (Will Smith) rivaled the Fat Boys with their lighthearted, curse-free raps, including "Parents Just Don't Understand" and "Girls Ain't Nothing But Trouble."

Jody Watley + Eric B. & Rakim   "Friends"

PHOTOGRAPHY: **Steven Meisel**
DESIGN: **Lynn Robb**
1989, MCA 1352, U.K.

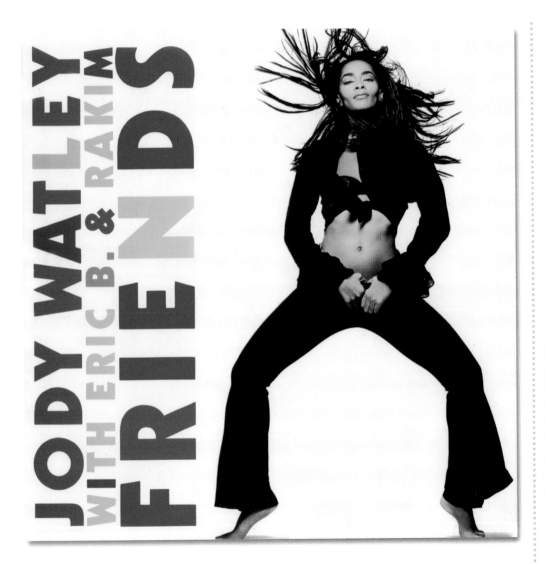

JODY WATLEY WITH ERIC B. & RAKIM FRIENDS

Jody Watley climbed the pop charts in '87 and '88 with singles such as "Looking for a New Love" and "Some Kind of Lover," culminating in an 1988 Best New Artist Grammy.

With one eye on her music and the other on style, cover artwork was always a focal point for Watley. Regarding "Friends": "I worked with legendary fashion photographer Steven Meisel on this photo session. I'd seen his layouts in Italian *Vogue*, and knew we would get timeless, iconic images. The photo we used for 'Friends' was the last set-up. I danced—he snapped—with wind machine in full effect!"

Jermaine Stewart

"Say It Again"

PHOTOGRAPHY: Marc Lebon
DESIGN: Bill Smith Studio
1987, 10 Records / SAYCD 188 {CD}, U.K.

Jody was also a longtime friend to Jermaine Stewart (of "We Don't Have to Take Our Clothes Off" fame). Both started their careers as *Soul Train* dancers and were involved with Shalamar before hitting their strides as successful solo artists.

| Limahl | "The Neverending Story" | PHOTOGRAPHY: Brian Aris
1984, EMI America 8230, U.S. |

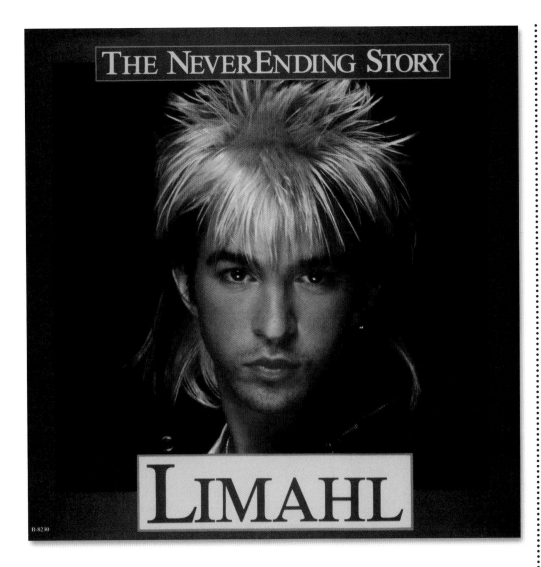

Look-alikes Limahl (originally with Kajagoogoo) and rock icon Rod Stewart sported their classic spiked hairdos on the sleeves for "The Neverending Story" and "Young Turks."

Fresh from his split from Kajagoogoo ("Too Shy"), Limahl joined forces with acclaimed producer Georgio Moroder for "The Neverending Story." It was his biggest solo hit.

Limahl recounts how "The Neverending Story" came together…barely: "I was at the Tokyo Music Festival about eight months before the movie was released and met Giorgio there. At this point 'Too Shy' was #1 all over the world. In Germany in particular, Kajagoogoo was enormously popular with teens and *The Neverending Story* was a bestselling children's book, so Giorgio saw the natural marketing potential. Not with the help of EMI, I might add. I remember my then manager Billy Gaff, an Irishman with a loud voice (and a short temper that he'd eloquently acquired by managing Rod Stewart in his heyday of 'Maggie May,' etc.) was literally shouting four letter words down the phone to then MD of EMI London Peter Jameson. He didn't believe in the song, regardless of its producer/writer credentials. Billy thankfully persuaded him by offering to pay for his first class air ticket to Germany to see the movie and hear the song in that context—a good tactic. EMI signed the soundtrack and it was a big seller for them worldwide."

Rod Stewart | "Young Turks" | DESIGN: Unknown
1981, Riva 34, U.K.

"When I flew into Germany to record the vocal, I had been out partying the night before and had a hangover. I was also a smoker back then (I didn't know any better at twenty-three years old), so the first few vocal takes were not happening, and I remember thinking, 'Shit, I'm gonna screw this up!' Had I known how important the song would become in my career and how it would affect my professional life I would have been in bed for 10 PM with a hot cup of cocoa. Anyway, Giorgio was the consummate professional, and said with his charming Italian accent, 'don't worry Lim—we'll have a little dinner then relax a little and try later.' Obviously the wine at dinner did the trick and, presto, I sailed through the vocal session, all thanks to a couple of glasses of German Red…or was it Italian…or maybe French?"

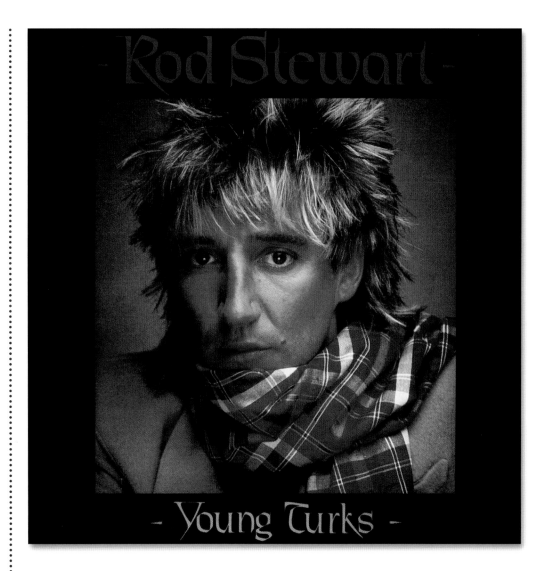

| Scorpions | "No Puedo Vivir Sin Ti" "(Can't Live without You)" | ARTWORK: Gottfried Helnwein 1982, EMI 064835, Spain |

The Scorpions were unparalleled in using provocative sleeves for their music. Their LPs from 1975 to 1980 (e.g., *Virgin Killer*, *Taken By Force*, *Animal Magnetism*) all caused panic at retail and with parents' groups.

When the band was discussing cover concepts for their *Blackout* LP and singles, including this Spanish sleeve for "Can't Live without You," artist Gottfried Helnwein caught the attention of Scorpions' lead singer Klaus Meine.

"There was a story on Gottfried Helnwein in a German magazine, and that's where I saw his 'self-portrait,' an image of a bandaged man being blinded," says Meine. "So, I went down to Vienna to meet with Helnwein at his studio, and asked him to add the shattering glass to make it a more powerful image. Helnwein liked the concept of being involved with a rock band and was really into the *Blackout* project. So, he painted the self-portrait again with the glass. It was perfect, exactly what we were looking for. It is interesting to note that in art books, sometimes you see Helnwein's original piece, and sometimes just the Scorpions cover when the 'self portrait' is discussed."

Meine continues, "After all these years, we still talk, and Helmwein mentioned that one day in 2003 or so Marilyn Manson showed up with the *Blackout* cover and wanted him to sign it. They later collaborated together [on Manson's *mOBSCENE* video, among other projects]."

| KISS | "Crazy Crazy Nights" | PHOTOGRAPHY: Walter Wick
1987, Mercury 888796, U.S. |

KISS' "Crazy Crazy Nights," also featuring a shattered glass cover, was recorded in the middle of the band's makeup-less period that stretched from '83 to '96. While the single struggled to gain traction in the U.S., it was KISS' biggest hit in the U.K. to date, reaching #4.

The Style Council   "Come to Milton Keynes"

PHOTOGRAPHY: Nick Knight
DESIGN: Paul Weller / Simon Halfon
1985, Polydor / TSCX 9 {12"}, U.K.

THE STYLE COUNCIL   COME TO MILTON KEYNES

"Come to Milton Keynes" and "Miles Away" both featured black-and-white shots of men's apparel.

Longtime Style Council/Paul Weller designer Simon Halfon on "Come to Milton Keynes": "That was one of my favourites. I directed a TV commercial [for The Style Council] and we got Rupert Everett, who was hot off his first feature *Another Country* (the poster of which featured prominently on the LP cover of *Our Favourite Shop*). Everett did the voice over, which parodied the Carlsberg Beer ad that was on television at the time. Instead of Orson Welles saying 'probably the best lager in the world,' Rupert said 'probably the best pop group in the world' over a lilting classical music background. Both Paul [Weller] and Mick [Talbot] only appeared in the commercial from behind, walking towards the coat stand in a static shot and picking up a copy of the album that sat at the bottom of the coat stand. The cover was a still from that shoot."

John Foxx

"Miles Away"

PHOTOGRAPHY: Herbie Yamaguchi
ART DIRECTION: John Foxx
1980, Virgin / VS 382, U.K.

MILES AWAY
John Foxx

Electronic pioneer John Foxx recounts "Miles Away": "The photograph was inspired by a Japanese horror film, *The H-Man*. I'd only seen a still from the film, an empty suit with something liquid leaving via the sleeve. The image gave me an entire set of images, connections, and stories, from the song "He's a Liquid," to some aspects of [my novel] *The Quiet Man*. When I saw an exhibition of [photographer] Cindy Sherman's work in New York, I got further confirmation of how accidental stories generated from exposure to forbidden film stills have inhabited our generation."

Milli Vanilli	"Blame It on the Rain"	PHOTOGRAPHY: **Esser & Strauss** DESIGN: **H. Wegner** 1989, Hansa 112364, Germany

Pop music's heavy emphasis on image boiled over in the late '80s with Milli Vanilli. Models Rob Pilatus and Fabrice Morvan were hired to front and lip-synch as Milli Vanilli to maximize the marketing appeal of the group. The scandal was eventually exposed, setting off a firestorm of bad publicity, not only for Milli Vanilli, but also for record labels and producers that encouraged style over substance.

In 1991 some of Milli Vanilli's original studio singers formed The Real Milli Vanilli and were seen for the first time. Despite being frequently discussed in the media, the vocalists behind Milli Vanilli have rarely been contacted regarding their story.

Charles Shaw, rapper on "Girl You Know It's True": "When I recorded 'Girl You Know Its True' for [producer] Frank Farian, I was told that it was only a DJ sampler, and after he developed it further with Rob and Fab, he said that if the project was successful he would use my voice for the whole album. Frank didn't keep his word. This didn't happen."

"I believe that too many recognized my voice due to my solo album *Hey You*. In Germany, nobody cared. However, once the song became a hit in the U.S. about a year later, and the group was nominated for a Grammy, Frank began to get concerned."

"When the story leaked to *Newsday* in the U.S. [December 14, 1989], Frank contacted me. He wanted to give me royalties. Right before the Grammy Awards in February, I signed a notarized agreement stating that I would never again claim that I was the lead voice on any Milli Vanilli song, and that I was simply a studio musician. He offered me 100,000 DM (about $55,000 USD). When Frank decided to tell the world the truth in the November '90 press conference, I was free to talk to the press again."

PHOTOGRAPHY: Simon Fowler
DESIGN: H. Wegner
1991, Hansa 614133 {12"}, Germany

"Frank never asked me to contribute to The Real Milli Vanilli, nor did he ask the two ladies who sang background on all of the Milli Vanilli songs—Jodie and Linda Rocco. Bottom line: not even The Real Millli Vanilli was the 'real' Milli Vanilli."

Milli Vanilli singer John Davis' story: "I met Frank at the Midem Music Festival in Cannes, France, and he gave me a deal as a solo singer. A few months later he asked me to come to the studio for a project that he was working on. So I went and got the job. He had a place with a studio upstairs and an apartment downstairs. I had to hide there, in the apartment, while the musicians recorded upstairs. I knew that something strange was going on. He later told me that I could make a lot of money with the situation, and said that he did another song with Charles Shaw, but was looking to add an additional voice."

"The night that the truth came out I was playing with my band in Europe, and the guys from Milli Vanilli called, asking that I start to sing with them on stage. Then Frank called and asked that I stick with him, and not to listen to anyone else who might phone. I sat with my band in the hotel room and was just laughing my ass off over the situation. I turned on the radio and realized that the situation had completely blown up."

"At about the same time I was on a show with Technotronic, and it was the same exact thing. There was this young girl on the microphone, and she wasn't singing shit."

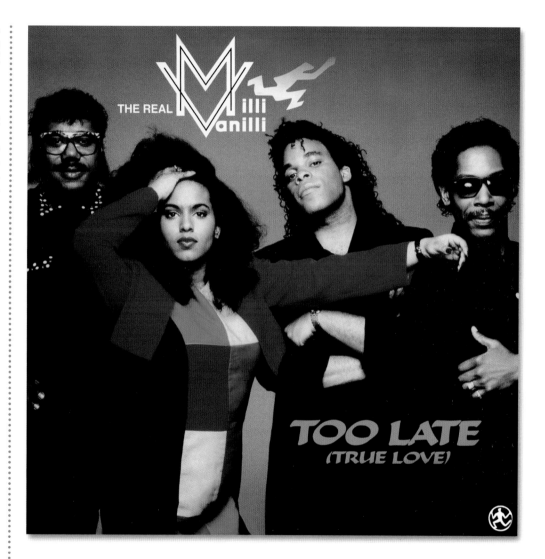

Technotronic	"Pump Up the Jam"	PHOTOGRAPHY: **Michel Poels**
		DESIGN: **Grafiek – Patrick**
		1989, SBK 07311, U.S.

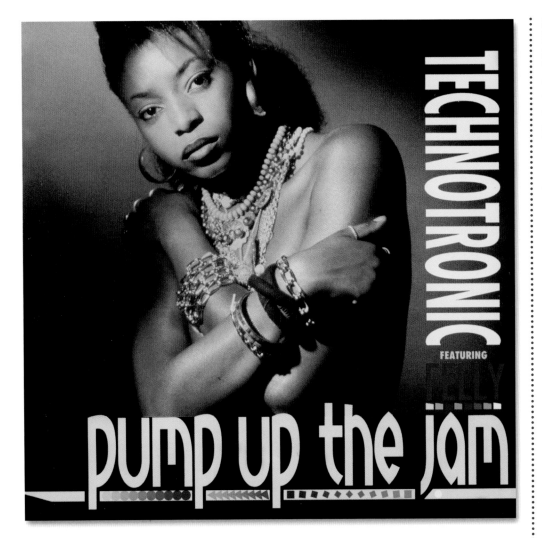

Similar to the Milli Vanilli scandal, African-born, non-English speaking model Felly was prominently featured on the single sleeve, video, and album cover for "Pump Up the Jam," but never recorded with the group.

The real Technotronic (Ya Kid K and MC Eric) were eventually brought to the forefront, as seen on their 1990 single "This Beat Is Technotronic."

Manuela Kamosi (Ya Kid K) recounts how "Pump Up the Jam" came together, including the Felly controversy: "In the mid-to-late '80s Jo Bogaert [founder of Technotronic] was releasing several anonymous records in the New Beat genre (a typical Belgian trend at the time—acid house records played at a slower speed). One of the records was named *Technotronik*, in essence an instrumental version of what later became 'Pump Up the Jam.' I was a feature rapper with the Belgian hip-hop crew Fresh Beat Production, as was handed an audio cassette of the track. I was told that the producer wanted to re-release the record with a black female rapper featured on it."

"The tape laid around in my room for quite some time, weeks or even months, and one day I decided to contrast the ultra synthetic sound of the instrumental with organic-sounding vocals (an African flow). My all-time favorite hip-hop track back then was Sweet Tee's 'It's My Beat,' which starts with 'The bass is thumpin', the party is jumpin', I got the rhymes to keep your body pumpin'… Those 'ump' words just did something for me, and within fifteen minutes I came up with the 'Pump Up the Jam' lyric."

"'Pump Up The Jam' created quite a buzz on the local scene, and before we knew it the song spread from territory to territory and became a hit. The initial intention for this track was that it would be a BeNeLux club hit."

"As I understand it, [model] Felly was signed to pretend to be the vocalist since I was refusing to sign any documents at the time (as I had no legal representation)…and because my look was not as marketable as a barely dressed model. I had later heard rumors within ARS Records that I was 'too ugly' to be on the sleeve. Without my knowledge or consent they printed her name on the sleeve as being the vocalist, had her do interviews in which she stated to be the vocalist, and recorded a music video with her lip syncing. All of a sudden, my voice belonged to another person."

"After realizing how upset I was, Bogaert assured me that it had been a mistake. I also put my foot down, appearing on local radio and performing the vocal live on the air. For 'Get Up! (Before the Night Is Over)' [originally slated to also 'feature' Felly], the record company decided to have both Felly and I in the video, so as not to shock the public but rather fade her out and fade me into the picture."

Despite the Felly controversy, Technotronic continued forward and had a series of hit singles. They even landed the coveted opening slot for Madonna's Blonde Ambition tour in '90. "Although I didn't quite understand how these simplistic songs had become such major hits on the pop scene," says Kamosi, "I did enjoy the star status for a while."

Kamosi eventually went solo and tended to personal affairs, but has continued working as a vocalist.

De La Soul brought alternative hip-hop to the mainstream. Their groundbreaking '89 LP, *3 Feet High and Rising*, mixed innovative sampling with positive wordplay, yielding masterpieces such as "Me Myself and I," "The Magic Number" (featuring a chorus from the kids show *Schoolhouse Rock!*), and "Eye Know."

3 Feet High and Rising also introduced De La Soul's "D.A.I.S.Y. age" visual concept. "D.A.I.S.Y. was an acronym for 'da inner sound, y'all'," says member Plug One (Kelvin Mercer), "our record company knew this could open us up to more people visually, so they came up with the idea of using colors and symbols from the '60s on our covers."

However, some fans were quick to peg De La Soul as "a trio of hippies," which irritated the group. "We tried an idea of having girls on stage, throwing out daisies at the end of our performances to symbolize 'Da Inner Sound,' and from there everyone took it literally," explains Plug One. De La Soul ended the concept with their next LP, *De La Soul Is Dead*, which featured a broken daisy flower pot on its cover. Despite the visual adjustment, the innovative music continued.

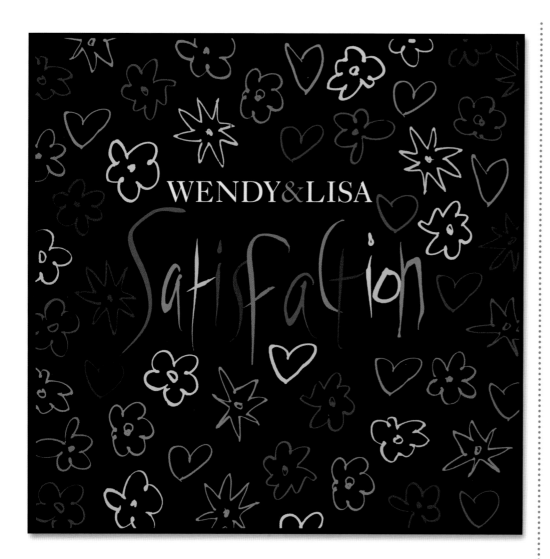

Similar to De La Soul, Wendy & Lisa tapped into vibrant imagery for their 1989 "Satisfaction" sleeve. "We were so lucky to meet Nick Egan, who we felt had a fantastic eye for design," says Lisa Coleman. "Nick came up with great iconographic images that were easily translated into what could be considered clip art. The 'Satisfaction' single is a perfect example. Egan ended up directing videos for us and became a dear friend."

| Michael Jackson | "Human Nature" | DESIGN: **Unknown** |
| | | 1983, Epic 04026, U.S. |

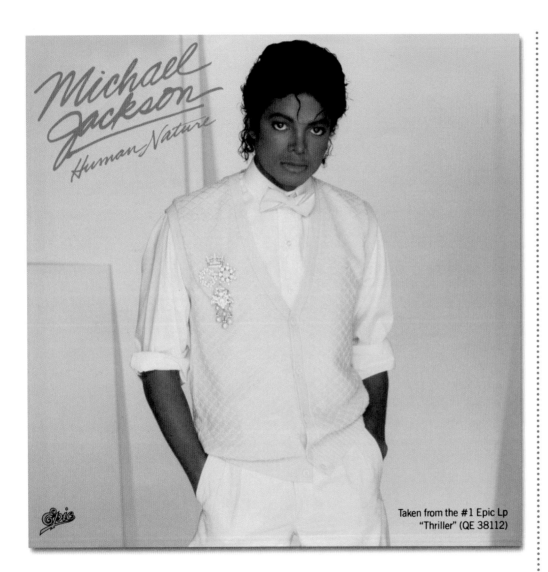

Taken from the #1 Epic Lp
"Thriller" (QE 38112)

"Human Nature" was the fifth consecutive U.S. Top 10 single from Michael Jackson's *Thriller*. The track, co-written by Toto's <u>Steve Porcaro</u>, was the last song selected for *Thriller* (ousting the Jackson-penned "Carousel"). "Human Nature's" smooth, brooding tempo helped set the tone for adult R&B in the mid-to-late '80s.

| La Toya Jackson | "Heart Don't Lie" | DESIGN: Unknown |
| | | 1984, Epic 4369, U.K. |

Following Michael Jackson' successes, sister La Toya cheekily recreated her brother's "Human Nature" outfit on her "Heart Don't Lie" release. The single, featuring backing vocals from Musical Youth ("Pass the Dutchie"), was a moderate success.

Before releasing the rock anthems "I Love Rock 'N Roll," "Crimson and Clover," and "I Hate Myself for Loving You," Joan Jett was first a guitarist and vocalist for the pioneering all-girl punk band The Runaways. Despite her success with the group, every major record label took a pass on Jett's debut solo LP *I Love Rock 'N Roll*. She subsequently co-founded Blackheart Records and shocked the industry when the album sold over ten million units worldwide.

"Weird Al" Yankovic	"I Love Rocky Road"	PHOTOGRAPHY: Sam Emerson
		ART DIRECTION: Al Yankovic
		1983, Rock 'n' Roll 03998, U.S.
		(*Courtesy of Jon "Bermuda" Schwartz*)

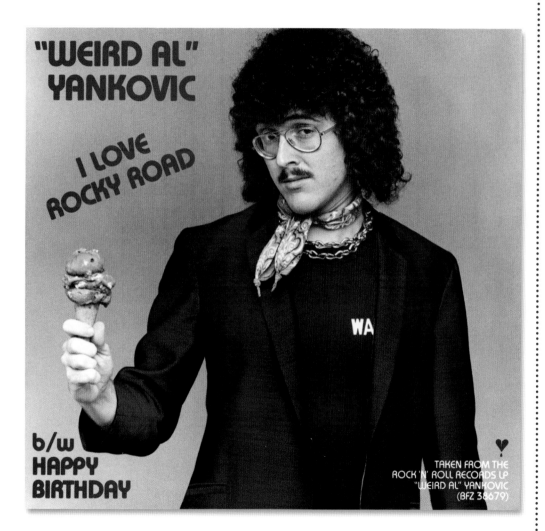

"'I Love Rock 'N Roll' was one of those rock anthems that virtually exploded out of radio—just a killer, monster riff," says "Weird Al" Yankovic, music's most successful satirist.

Yankovic not only parodied some of the '80s most popular songs and videos (including Michael Jackson's "Beat It" ["Eat It"] and Madonna's "Like a Virgin" ["Like a Surgeon"]), but he also recreated the related single covers. Here he mimicked the sleeve for "I Love Rock 'N Roll," including the font, jacket, blue scarf, double chain, and two exposed letters (changing his to "WA" for "Weird Al").

"I don't think we had much of a budget for the single cover art, since I wasn't really an established artist at this point," says Yankovic. "Nowadays I would obsessively recreate the exact wardrobe and color-match everything, but for this shoot I think I just grabbed some horrible old suit jacket out of my closet and figured it was close enough."

Yankovic continues, "It was a huge song for Joan Jett and an obvious choice for a parody target. Granted, 'I Love Rocky Road' is far from being the cleverest variation on a theme I've ever done, but hey—I was going through my 'food phase.' I've bumped into Joan once or twice since 1983, and she's never sucker-punched me, so I guess she's okay with the parody."

But did Al *really* love rocky road ice cream? "I've always been fond of rocky road, but truthfully, after all the promotional ice cream-eating contests I was involved in after the release of the record, I was pretty sick of that particular flavor for a while," quips Yankovic.

'Do They Know It's Christmas?'

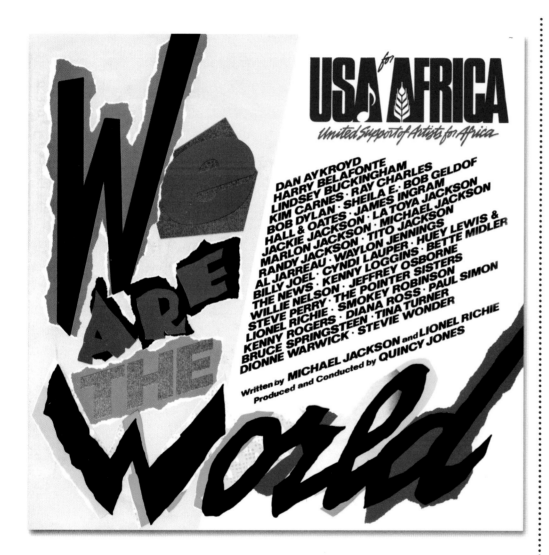

The '80s string of charity singles began with the British music coalition Band Aid, which included Culture Club, Wham!, Spandau Ballet, Bananarama, and Sting, among others. The single cover was by Peter Blake, best known for designing the artwork for the Beatles' *Sgt. Pepper's Lonely Hearts Club Band*.

The United States responded with its own musical supergroup for famine relief, USA for Africa (see the single cover for its huge stateside cast).

Other fundraisers followed, such as Artists United Against Apartheid's "Sun City," Dionne and Friends' "That's What Friends Are For" (which benefited AIDS research), and Voices of America's "Hands Across America" (supporting the homeless).

BOB GELDOF

THIS IS THE WORLD CALLING

Live Aid organizer Bob Geldof and Farm Aid co-founder John Cougar (Mellencamp) appear here in "framed" black-and-white portraits.

Watched by an estimated 1.5 billion people in 100 countries, Live Aid was a multi-venue concert held on July 13, 1985, to raise awareness and funds for famine relief in Ethiopia. A who's who of musicians performed, including sets by Queen, U2, David Bowie, Madonna, Mick Jagger with Tina Turner, Run-D.M.C., Duran Duran, and Phil Collins (who played both in the U.K. and the U.S.).

Following comments made by Bob Dylan at Live Aid about the plight of the U.S. farmer, a Farm Aid benefit concert was coordinated by John Mellencamp and Willie Nelson on September 22, 1985. Farm Aid continued annually, with regular performers such as Neil Young and the Dave Matthews Band.

NEW KIDS ON THE BLOCK

this one's for the children

The holidays are simply not complete without hearing seasonal '80s favorites such as Wham!'s "Last Christmas," Madonna's "Santa Baby," and Hall and Oates' "Jingle Bell Rock." Nearly every mainstream artist was either contributing to a holiday compilation (see the Very Special Christmas *series) or churning out their own album of holiday standards (New Kids on the Block, etc.).*

The Waitresses had their own holiday classic in "Christmas Wrapping" (not shown). At the time, founding member Chris Butler wasn't too fond of the holidays.

"I was such a Scrooge that some pals made me a t-shirt that read, 'JUMP, GEORGE BAILEY, JUMP!' Still have it, too," says Butler. "The song blind-sides me every year. I'm running around like a lunatic, and it will spill out of a shoe store at the mall or come on the radio, and it makes me slow down and go 'yeah…Christmas…nice.'"

The Bangles	"In Your Room"	PHOTOGRAPHY:	Sheila Rock
		ART DIRECTION:	Tony Lane / Nancy Donald
		DESIGN:	Lesley Schiff
			1988, Columbia 08090, U.S.

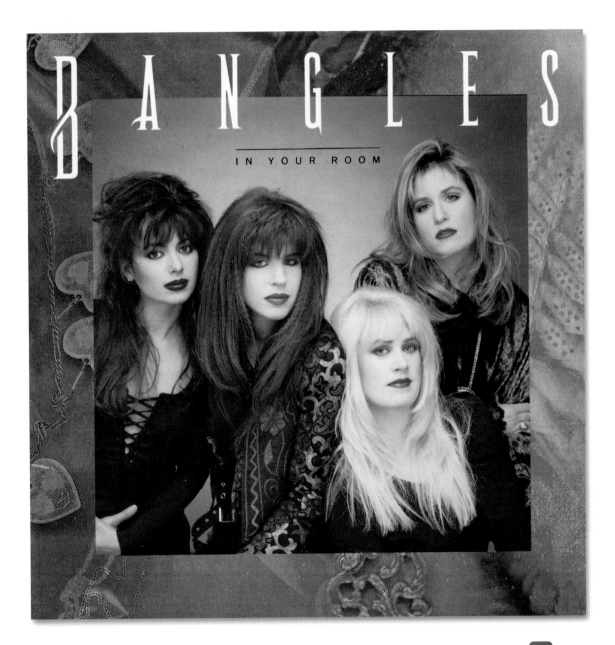

Heart	"Alone"	DESIGN: Unknown
		1987, Capitol 44002, U.S.

Sisters are doin' it for themselves.

Siblings Ann and Nancy Wilson led Heart to several '80s anthems ("These Dreams," "Alone"), while sisters Debbi and Vicki Peterson helped bring The Bangles ("Eternal Flame," "In Your Room") into the spotlight.

Both beat the odds in a male-dominated rock music scene.

"We never paid too much attention to the obstacles we faced," says The Bangles' Susanna Hoffs, "The struggle was part of the experience. We did not feel that being female artists was novel in any way. After all, we came of age in the '70s and were inspired by great female singers like Joni Mitchell, Bonnie Raitt, Carole King, and Patti Smith."

Unlike many of today's young female artists, "The Bangles controlled our own style and image," remarks Hoffs. "In the very early days we'd scour thrift stores for vintage '60s clothes, and even had things made for us since it was so hard to find the mod, Carnaby Street clothes that we loved. It wasn't until we signed with Columbia that we had access to stylists and makeup artists. Suddenly, there was a pressure to look a certain way, but we learned to assert ourselves in those situations. I still cringe looking at many old photos from the '80s. Enough time has passed that it is actually starting to be fun to look back on those crazy outfits and fashion faux pas."

The Bangles' hit "In Your Room" was co-written by Hoffs. "I remember hearing Tommy James & The Shondells' 'Mony Mony' and mentioning to Billy [Steinberg, co-writer] that it would be fun to write something with the energy and spirit of that song. The goal was to write a song that captured the elation of being in love, an almost indescribable feeling."

Tracey Ullman	"They Don't Know"	PHOTOGRAPHY: Simon Fowler / Clare Muller
		DESIGN: Geoff Gans
		1983, MCA / Stiff 52347, U.S.

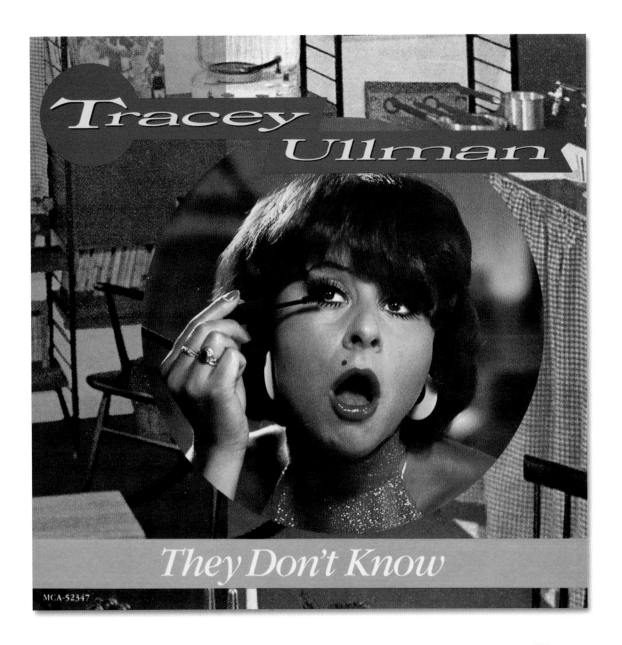

Eddie Murphy	"Party All the Time"	PHOTOGRAPHY: Lynn Goldsmith
		DESIGN: Nancy Greenberg
		1985, Columbia 05609, U.S.

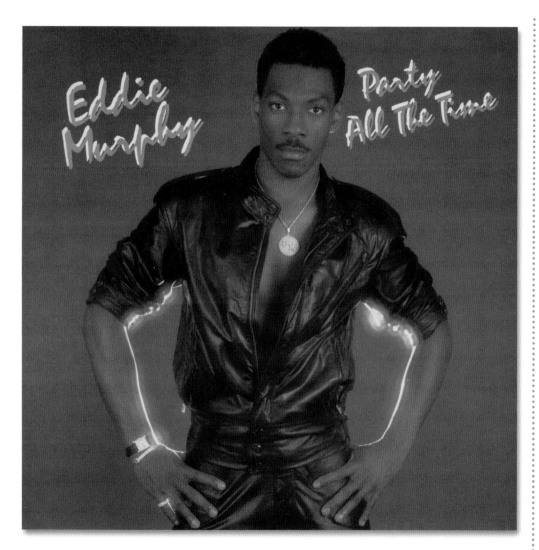

Comedians Tracey Ullman and Eddie Murphy scored hit singles with "They Don't Know" and "Party All the Time" (produced by Rick James).

"They Don't Know" showcased Tracey's retro '60s music style, whereas "Party All the Time" showed off Murphy's R&B pipes, which he typically delegated to Saturday Night Live skits such as "Little Richard Simmons" and "James Brown's Celebrity Hot Tub Party."

Other comedians that crossed over to radio in the '80s included Rodney Dangerfield ("Rappin' Rodney"), Billy Crystal ("You Look Mahvelous"), and Bob and Doug McKenzie ("Take Off").

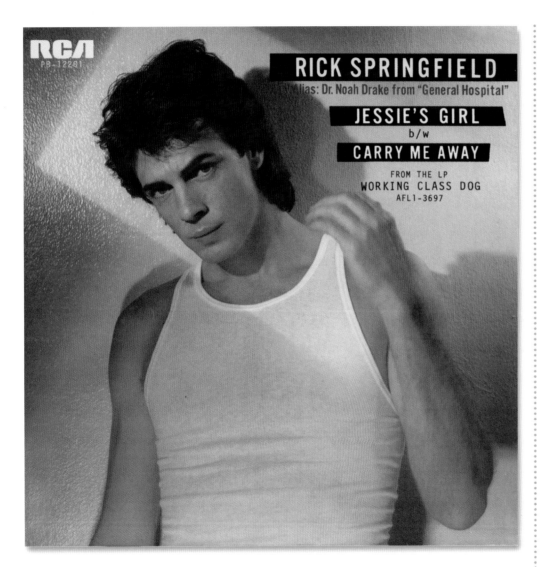

From the small screen to the turntable: General Hospital*'s* ***"Dr. Noah Drake"*** *(Rick Springfield)* and *Miami Vice's* ***"Sonny Crockett"*** *(Don Johnson) both found success at radio with* ***"Jessie's Girl"*** *and* ***"Heartbeat."***

After hitting #1 in the U.S. with "Jessie's Girl," Rick left his popular role on *General Hospital* to focus on his music. Some DJs hesitated to play Rick's songs due to his teen idol image.

"There's a downside to everything, but there's also an upside," says Springfield. "I never actively did anything with the teen mags in the '80s. They just used interviews from when I first came to America in the early '70s and put more current photos with the articles. It helped in that teenage fans have the loudest voice when it comes to up and coming bands, but it also limited people's view of me. For a lot of critics I was perceived as a one dimensional figure that wouldn't be around for very long. I think the only redress is sticking along long enough to disprove them."

Springfield went on to chart an impressive sixteen U.S. Top 40 hits from 1981 to 1988, including "I've Done Everything for You," "Don't Talk to Strangers," and "Love Somebody."

Springfield battled with RCA over the *Working Class Dog* LP album cover art. RCA wanted to use the photo from the "Jessie's Girl" single (shown here), while Springfield opted for a tongue-in-cheek image of his dog Ron. Springfield won the argument.

"My idea was always to have my dog, Lethal Ron, on the LP cover," says Springfield, "because he was much cooler than me, but I had to fight RCA for it. The record execs couldn't get past the idea of having a budding television star on the cover, but I insisted, and they eventually agreed to put my photo on the back. They did do about 10,000 reverse covers of the LP with me on the front, but everyone complained and they had to switch it back. The original cover eventually got nominated for best album cover at that year's Grammy Awards, so there was some vindication for me and my dog."

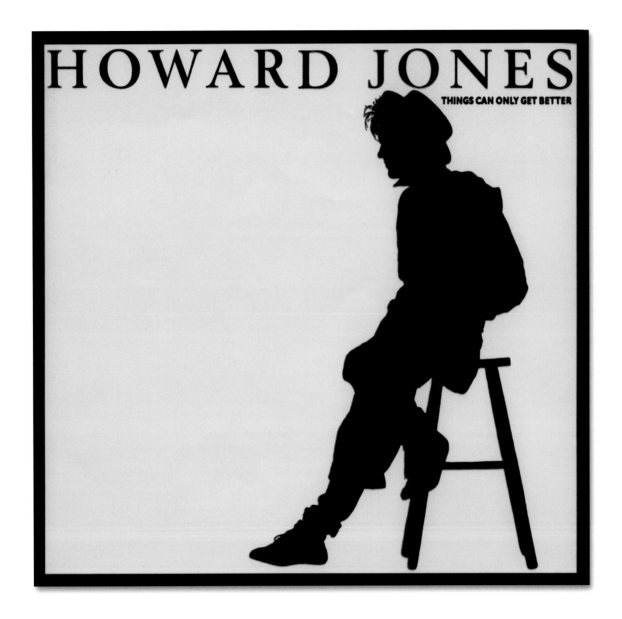

Information Society

"What's on Your Mind
(Pure Energy)"

PHOTOGRAPHY: Isabel Snyder
ART DIRECTION: The Grey Organisation
DESIGN: Steven Miglio
1988, Tommy Boy 27826, U.S.

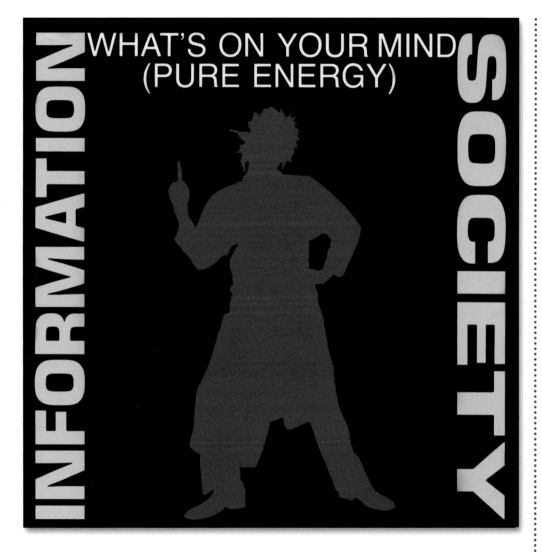

A silhouette graphic was used for "Things Can Only Get Better" and "What's on Your Mind (Pure Energy)." The outlines of Howard Jones and Kurt Harland of Information Society are instantly recognizable due to their avant-garde hair and clothing.

Information Society's Paul Robb: "All of our cover art from the era (as well as the art direction for the first few videos) reflected our obsession with bright primary covers at the time. Before we moved to New York, when we were an unsigned local band in Minneapolis, we wore these custom-made two-tone jumpsuits with the same sort of bright, primary colors. Even on our last tour as a threesome (in 1993), we all wore outfits made from day-glo orange hunters' fabric. I think we simply absorbed the love of bright colors which was in the air during our formative, new wave years."

"We were TV-obsessed slackers during that whole period," continues Robb. "One of the things Kurt liked to do was record TV shows—*Kung Fu*, *Scooby Doo*, and especially *Star Trek* in order to get the sound effects. He had made a large library of these samples, and when we were doing preproduction on the first record, I popped several of them into songs, including the infamous 'pure energy' sample." Spock said the phrase in the *Star Trek* episode "Errand of Mercy."

"We never did meet Leonard Nimoy," says Robb, "but his son, Adam Nimoy, was a friend of an A&R man at Warner Brothers, and it was Adam who played the record for his dad, explaining that we were being squashed like bugs between the millstones of Warner Communications and Paramount Pictures over the rights to the *Star Trek* samples. Apparently, Leonard felt enough pity for us that he offered to actually re-record the line if Paramount would not give us the rights, and this broke the logjam and allowed us to use those samples."

Cher	"I Found Someone"	PHOTOGRAPHY: Matthew Rolston
		DESIGN: Gabrielle Raumberger
		1987, Geffen 28191, U.S.

Cher and Taylor Dayne, here in similar head shots, both understood the power of strong imagery and style.

"Cher was a dream to work with," says sleeve designer Gabrielle Raumberger, "very down to earth and receptive to collaborating on ideas for the project. We went on location to the alley behind Pantages Theatre in Hollywood, where Matthew Rolston shot beautiful, gritty black-and-white images with Cher wearing her signature black leather jacket. At the time, I loved hand tinting black-and-white photos, so I showed Cher my technique on a few of the images and she loved it, so we used them for the album [and single] package. Also, the song titles were written in my handwriting, so the cover feels all the more personal to me. It should also be noted that the image for 'I Found Someone' was originally slotted for the related album cover, but Cher decided to switch them last minute."

| Taylor Dayne | "Don't Rush Me" | DESIGN: Ariola-Studios / Aaron's Outfit
1988, Arista 111687, U.K. |

"Image is so important to music," says Taylor Dayne, "just ask that little blonde girl from Detroit [Madonna]. I always fight for the opportunity to work with the greatest fashion photographers and video directors." This included video director Dominic Sena, who went on to helm *Gone in 60 Seconds* and *Swordfish*, among other films.

Salt-N-Pepa	"Push It"	PHOTOGRAPHY:	Janette Beckman
		DESIGN:	Jeff Faville
		LOGO:	Christopher Martin
			1988, FFRR 886250, France

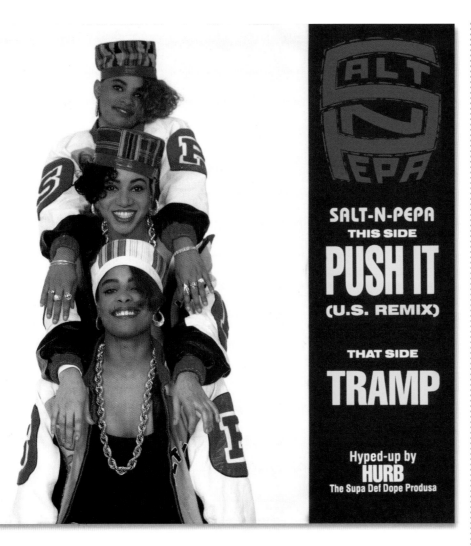

SALT-N-PEPA
THIS SIDE

PUSH IT
(U.S. REMIX)

THAT SIDE

TRAMP

Hyped-up by
HURB
The Supa Def Dope Produsa

Salt-N-Pepa and Kid 'N Play went against the hardcore rap trends and created positive, socially conscious music.

Christopher Martin ("Play") on the origins of Kid 'N Play and Salt-N-Pepa: "I was very much the street wannabe, looking for ways to get in trouble to increase my rep on the streets, and Kid at that time was a student at the Bronx High School of Science, where he was the bookworm. He used to amaze me. When I was over his house and *Jeopardy* was on he would literally know all the answers."

"So, there was a big party that was happening in the neighborhood, and Kid's voice stood out to me and my friends. We were amazed, because he looked nothing like the voice that was on the microphone. He had thick, horn-ripped glasses—a complete nerd."

Kid 'N Play and Salt-N-Pepa, along with Salt/Kid producer Hurby "Love Bug" Azor and comedian Martin Lawrence all worked together at Sears in Queens, New York, before hitting it big.

Kid 'N Play	"Gittin' Funky"	PHOTOGRAPHY: Kevin Davies
		DESIGN: John Pasche
		1988, Cooltempo 168, U.K.

"Kid and I were already friends, so I hooked Kid up with the job. Then there was Hurby, Cheryl ['salt'], Sandie ['Pepa'], and Martin Lawrence. Herby was working on a class project for a trade school, and he had an audio/technology assignment. So he decided to do a record with Cheryl and Sandie [*The Showstopper*, an answer record to Doug E. Fresh's *The Show*]." They were known as Supernature for this initial release, and then switched to Salt-N-Pepa, the first all-female rap crew that broke into the mainstream.

At the same time, Kid 'N Play opened the floodgates for casting hip-hop artists in film and on television. *House Party* (starring Kid 'N Play, Martin Lawrence, Full Force, and Robin Harris) was a smash at the box office, spawning several sequels. "When it ended up a hit it was a complete surprise to me—still to this day. I was hesitant to take the role because the rap movies of the era were hit and miss. I was outvoted. I'm glad I lost," says Martin.

"Ultimately, I think what resonated from us the most was the fun we liked to have. Kid, Salt, Pep, and I are still friends."

gittin' funky

WHEN THE CHILDREN CRY

Survivor's "Eye of the Tiger" and White Lion's "When the Children Cry" had rival feline covers.

Sylvester Stallone commissioned Survivor to write "Eye of the Tiger" for *Rocky III*. It was an immediate, iconic anthem, even receiving an Oscar nomination for Best Original Song. Survivor delivered another hit with the *Rocky IV* hit "Burning Heart."

Survivor founding member Frankie Sullivan: "Sylvester Stallone was a friend of Tony Scotti, who ran Scotti Brothers Records. There was another song in *Rocky III*, Queen's "Another One Bites the Dust," but Stallone wanted something new. Tony mentioned us."

"At that time I was really young, and I don't really think I really realized what it meant, but I nevertheless was very excited. We wrote the music in about ten or fifteen minutes. Jim [Peterik] and I then worked on the lyrics for two to three days."

"At the same time we also wrote a ballad called 'Ever Since the World Began,' and that was our favorite. So our demo for Stallone had both of the songs together, and we discounted 'Eye' a bit. Stallone ended up going nuts when he heard 'Tiger' (and later ended up using the other song at the end of his film *Lock Up*)."

"When I went to see *Rocky III* in a regular theater with an audience, people clapped after the opening montage with the song. I think that's when it hit me that we were onto something big."

Sheena Easton	"Sugar Walls"	PHOTOGRAPHY: Brian Aris
		ART DIRECTION: Henry Marquez
		DESIGN: Carol Chen
		1984, EMI America 8253, U.S.

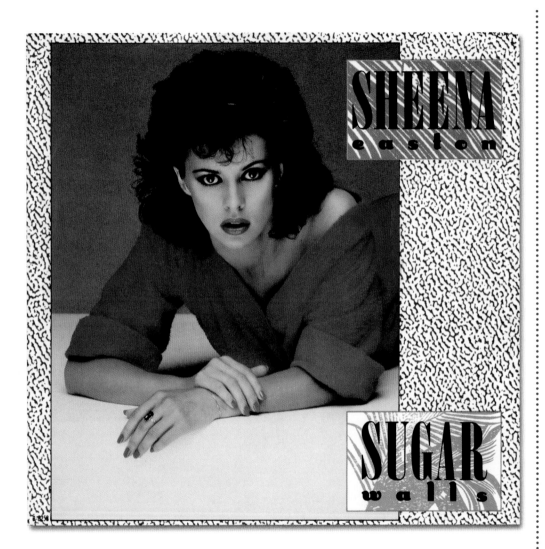

Normally chaste vocalists Sheena Easton and Gloria Estefan turned up the heat with "Sugar Walls" and "Bad Boy."

Easton's "Sugar Walls" was composed by Alexander Nevermind (a.k.a. Prince). His provocative lyrics landed the song on the PMRC's infamous "Filthy Fifteen" list, alongside other "dirty" tracks such as "Darling Nikki" (Prince), "Dress You Up" (Madonna), and "She Bop" (Cyndi Lauper). The *Sugar Walls* video was even banned by some video outlets based on the song's lyrical content alone.

"Bad Boy" was Miami Sound Machine's follow-up to their breakthrough smash "Conga." By 1989, Gloria Estefan was credited as a solo artist, while the changing lineup of Miami Sound Machine continued as her backing band.

| Tiffany | "I Saw Him Standing There" | PHOTOGRAPHY: Randee St. Nicholas 1988, MCA 53285, U.S. |

| Debbie Gibson | "Lost in Your Eyes" | PHOTOGRAPHY: Albert Watson
1989, Atlantic 88970, U.S. |

Teen queens Tiffany and Debbie Gibson dominated the '80s airwaves while maintaining clean-cut, "girl next door" images. Tiffany ruled the "mall chicks" while Debbie Gibson presided over the "electric youth."

Gibson explains the difficult road to stardom for young singers in the '80s, "I was self sufficient as a writer and producer," explains Gibson. "One hundred songs were written and recorded before Atlantic agreed to sign me to a dance single deal. I then played three shows a night, four nights a week while attending high school. I played clubs across the USA and got it goin' grass roots."

Looking back at the "Lost in Your Eyes" artwork, Gibson states that "I was into acting my age and being authentic. I fought hard for that. Everyone wanted to sex me up. I loved hats, and…apparently…loved to pout."

In an era of manufactured teen images in the recording industry, Gibson's advice for impending pop stars is straight-forward: "A label will make you feel like you're at their mercy. Sex sells records, but only if it comes from an organic place. So, if that's your thing—cool. If not, don't force it. You will attract an audience by being true to yourself. Also, arm yourself with the knowledge of writing, producing, and the business side of things. Being a dumb blonde chick singer is *such* a cliché!"

Debbie Gibson and Tiffany joined forces and toured together in 2011.

XTC	"This World Over"	DESIGN: Andy Partridge 1984, Virgin / VS 721, U.K.

XTC
THIS WORLD OVER

XTC's Andy Partridge: "I love sleeves that have a sense of 'event' to them, sleeves that do something, and don't just lay there. Any sleeve I turn my hand to has to slide out, unfold, be 3-D, have extra sections, etc. This one was no exception."

"The perspiration behind this sleeve was *that* famous photo of Hiroshima, after the bomb, just showing the city street system with piles of rubble laid between them. All was gone. Of course, this song was from the '80s, the high, heavy water mark of nuclear paranoia everywhere, but the only cultural reference anyone had was those WWII events."

"Twigging that if we did get involved in a nuclear Armageddon than every city in the world was going to end up looking the same, I thought that a set of postcards from a selection of cities should be included. We used identical pictures, touched up to the max with fake blue sky, and presented them in a drop down set. The sort of selection you could find on any turnaround stand in any holiday venue. The point being that as soon as we enter into nuclear lunacy, all the major cities in the world will become identical in their destruction."

"XTC bassist Colin Moulding contributed a quirky touch. He thought that we should add the request 'stop' button, found on older English buses and familiar from our childhoods, to the package. The button had a sign with it saying 'push once.' The very instruction that was surely needed if it had of been an actual nuclear button."

"The packaging won an award in the U.K., but as usual I didn't get it and wasn't invited to the ceremony. This still goes on today. Oh well, onwards and upwards, just back away from that button."

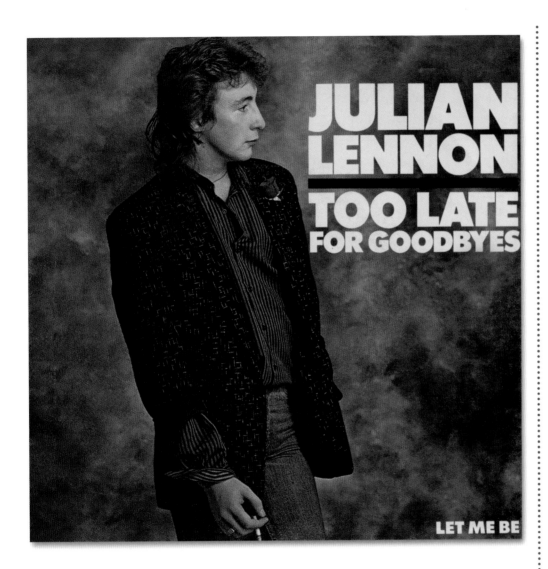

John Lennon's first born, Julian, followed his father's footsteps with a solo career of his own in the mid-'80s, including the single "Too Late for Goodbyes."

The prophetically titled "I'm Stepping Out" was recorded just prior to John Lennon's untimely passing on December 8, 1980. The cover photo showed John shaving with Sean, his son with Yoko Ono.

"It is too painful for me to comment on the cover of this single, in which Sean is innocently looking up at his dad," says Ono. "Neither one of them knew what fateful event was waiting for them. I hope one day soon, we will all live in a world without violence."

| ZZ Top | "Velcro Fly" | DESIGN: A.D. Consultants |
| | | 1986, Warner 8650, U.K. |

VELCRO® FLY

ZZ Top's "Velcro Fly" had just that, a real velcro fly on the sleeve, while Madonna's limited edition version of "Express Yourself" had a zipper crotch closure (the backside of the sleeve is shown here).

Both covers seemed inspired by Andy Warhol's LP design for *Sticky Fingers* (The Rolling Stones, 1971), which had a close-up of Mick Jagger's package and a working zipper fly.

Madonna

"Express Yourself"

DESIGN: Warner U.K.
1989, Sire 2948 (zipper bag), U.K.
{backside of 7" sleeve}

side one
express yourself

side two
the look of love

The End

Maybe you can't always judge a record by its cover, but let's face it, you usually can.

I am unable to think of a record I ever bought without finding something aesthetically pleasing about the design of the sleeve. It is possible that, on a rare occasion, I may have turned a blind eye to a dodgy typeface or perhaps even forgiven the over enthusiastic cropping of a photograph, but in general, I am simply drawn to the things I find appealing.

Historically this method of rapid visual elimination has conserved an enormous amount of my time. Seem a little harsh? Well, let me explain my rules of attraction. The kind of music I like has always been made by stylish mavericks—those with a unique approach. This manner of thinking is rarely limited to auditory creation; these are the people who obsess over every detail in life. I can often spot them from afar, but everything always comes into sharp focus once I see their artwork. It is

the design choices they make, their collaborators, and of course the final image which purveys so much about their character. The record cover is a catalyst to intrigue: Who are they? Where do they come from? What do they sound like? I would surmise that an appropriate design could comfortably give more than a hint as to the music contained therein.

In a decade scorned for its extravagance and frivolity, many fail to recognize the unrestrained experimentation, innovation, vibrancy, and diversity, which truly defined its character. Those who rejoiced as the doors slammed shut on the '80s seemed confident that the future was sure to deliver substance and meaningful change. Well maybe it did for some, but the DNA of what was to follow had already crystallized in the preceding years. From the birth of MTV and supermodels, to hip-hop and style magazines, pop culture exploded in beautiful colours. You dressed to impress and weren't afraid to embrace success. This was a time

before our sphere was homogenized by reality TV, before mediocre seemed daring. Amidst the creative chaos, we saw the fall of the Berlin wall and the humble beginnings of the World Wide Web. There was a startling energy and new ideas burst open the days with fearless aplomb.

Regarding graphic design, there was no Photoshop, so what you saw was much closer to the truth; handmade with love and attitude.

It becomes evident when you have leafed through this blithely curated collection of singles artwork that each individual cover is a declaration of style, or lack of it—a personal statement of intent, a tiny billboard, passionately advertising a product, and now a frozen moment. Whether subtle or brash, chic or kitsch, together they form a provocative document from an era of grand gestures.

Nick Rhodes
LONDON, FEBRUARY 2011

Acknowledgments

The author would like to thank the following people for their assistance with this book...

Much love to my mom, dad, brother, and sister, for always being there, and for putting up with my mild music obsession over the years. When I was hoarding vinyl, CDs, posters, and music mags, you walked over them with a smile. That's family.

Brian Jasinski, Popp Twinn extraordinaire. Thanks for the friendship and creative support. I couldn't have done it without you.

To Roger Zender, Cleveland's biggest ally and best resource for indie music...and an all-around fantastic guy. Thanks for all of the advice and for being such a great ear. Here's to the Barking Spider and beyond!

Chris Hamilton, your early support and ideas were really appreciated, and helped to get this project off the ground.

Jake Shears, I'm still pinching myself. As I was daydreaming about who I would like to write the foreword, you were always on the top of my list. I reached out and you responded within a few days. Thank you so much, and stay ballsy.

Perhaps nobody knows the art and music worlds better than Nick Rhodes. You were at the forefront of merging genre-defining music with brilliant visuals, and are still leading the way. Thank you for taking time out of your busy schedule to contribute.

To all of my friends, from the '80s and thereafter, and to everyone at Schiffer, you are first class all the way.

Thanks also to the recording and cover artists that I interviewed for the book. I appreciate your incredible stories, as well as your phenomenal music and artwork over the years:

Andie Airfix, Neil Arthur/Blancmange, Martyn Atkins, Jules Balme, Frankie Banali/Quiet Riot, Toni Basil, Lou Beach, Robyn Beeche, Andy Bell/Erasure, Bow Wow Wow, Boy Meets Girl, Buckner & Garcia, John Carder Bush, Chris Butler/The Waitresses, Gerald Casale/Devo, Catherine Chambaret, Christopher Ciccone, Josie Cotton, Bob Dalton/It Bites, Clark Datchler/Johnny Hates Jazz, John Davis, Martha Davis/Motels, Thomas Dolby, Dead Milkmen, Ivan Doroschuk/Men Without Hats, Geoff Downes & John Wetton/Asia, Corrine Drewery/Swing Out Sister, Doug Fieger/The Knack, Samantha Fox, John Foxx, Martin Fry/ABC, Per Gessle/Roxette, Deborah Gibson, Yvonne Gilbert, Robbie Grey/Modern English, Simon Halfon, Jan Hammer, Paul Hardcastle, Corey Hart, Thomas Hauck & Fred Pineau/The Atlantics, Doug Henders, Mike Hodges, Susanna Hoffs/The Bangles, Mark Holmes/Platinum Blonde, Scott Ian/Anthrax, Tony James/Sigue Sigue Sputnik, The Jets, J.J. Fad, Andy Johnson, Lauren Johnson/Book of Love, Manuela Kamosi/Technotronic, Jay King, Jan Kuehnemund/Vixen, Simon LeBon & John Taylor/Duran Duran, Betty LeBron/Sweet Sensation, Johnny Lee, Annie Lennox, Limahl, Laura LiPuma-Nash, Sananda Maitreya, Mary Jane Girls, James Marsh, Christopher Martin/Kid 'N Play, Andy McCluskey/OMD, Darryl McDaniels/Run-D.M.C., Meco, Kelvin Mercer/De La Soul, Klaus Meine/Scorpions, Mark Morales & Damon Wimbley/Fat Boys, Dennis Morris, Jill Mumford, Musical Youth, Margo Nahas, Helen Namm, Melanie Nissen, Gary Numan, Terri Nunn/Berlin, Rob O'Connor, Yoko Ono, Andy Partridge/XTC, Mike Patterson, Slim Jim Phantom/The Stray Cats, Edwin Pouncey, Rammellzee, Gabrielle Raumberger, Derek Riggs, James Rizzi, Paul Robb/Information Society, Liz Rosenberg, Gerald Scarfe, Inge Schaap, Fred Schneider/The B-52's, Rocky Schenck, Charles Shaw, Jimmy Somerville, Rick Springfield, Frankie Sullivan/Survivor, Rod Swenson/The Plasmatics, Kathy Valentine/The Go-Go's, Bruce Vilanch, Martyn Ware/Heaven 17, James Warren/The Korgis, Jody Watley, Eric Watson, Mark Weiss, Wendy & Lisa, Robert Williams, "Weird Al" Yankovic, and Young MC.

FINALLY, THANKS TO YOU FOR READING.

Index of Artists

Index of Artists

Index of Artists

Index of Artists

Index of Artists

Index of Artists

Every attempt was made to acknowledge the cover artists for each featured sleeve. Please contact the author if you know of additional credits that should be included in future editions of this book.

Questions and comments for the author can be mailed to **matthew@matthewchojnacki.com**

www.**matthewchojnacki**.com

A portion of all sales benefit the Keep a Child Alive Foundation.